Jerusalem

The Story of a Song

Jerusalem

The Story of a Song

Edwin Lerner

Winchester, UK
Washington, USA

JOHN HUNT PUBLISHING

First published by Chronos Books, 2022
Chronos Books is an imprint of John Hunt Publishing Ltd., No. 3 East St., Alresford,
Hampshire SO24 9EE, UK
office@jhpbooks.com
www.johnhuntpublishing.com
www.chronosbooks.com

For distributor details and how to order please visit the 'Ordering' section on our website.

ISBN: 978 1 80341 104 0
978 1 80341 105 7 (ebook)
Library of Congress Control Number: 2021949286

A CIP catalogue record for this book is available from the British Library.

Design: Stuart Davies

UK: Printed and bound by CPI Group (UK) Ltd, Croydon, CR0 4YY
Printed in North America by CPI GPS partners

We operate a distinctive and ethical publishing philosophy in
all areas of our business, from our global network of authors to
production and worldwide distribution.

Contents

To Henry and Julia

And did those feet in ancient time,
Walk upon England's mountains green?
And was the holy Lamb of God
On England's pleasant pastures seen?
And did the Countenance Divine
Shine forth upon our clouded hills?
And was Jerusalem builded here,
Among these dark Satanic Mills?
Bring me my bow of burning gold:
Bring me my Arrows of desire:
Bring me my Spear: O clouds unfold:
Bring me my Chariot of Fire!
I will not cease from Mental Fight,
Nor shall my Sword sleep in my hand:
Till we have built Jerusalem,
In England's green & pleasant Land.

William Blake

Acknowledgements

I am grateful to the many people who have helped me in the preparation of this book. The idea came to me after I was invited to visit the house in Sussex where William and Catherine Blake lived and where he probably wrote the words which make up the song that we call *Jerusalem* – although he never called it by that name. For Blake, *Jerusalem* was the name of a much longer poem, subtitled *Emanation of the Giant Albion*.

I hope that plans to open the house are progressing and, by the time you read this, we are able to go inside this attractive flint-lined thatched house in Felpham near Bognor Regis. I am also grateful to everyone at the Blake Society who have answered my persistent questions and given me greater insight into this important and often misunderstood man.

David Russell and his wife, the great-granddaughter of Hubert Parry, provided much useful information and great hospitality when I visited them at Shulbrede Priory and I was privileged to enjoy not only their excellent fruit cake and tea (made with tea leaves, I noted) but was able to see the original manuscript of Parry's score for the musical setting of Blake's poem, which he wrote in the darkest days of the First World War, laconically noting in his diary that the weather was "damp and cold".

Blake has many admirers and I am thankful to all those who shared their thoughts on this eccentric and difficult but much-loved man. The pianist Chris Dann, like many lovers of Blake's work, expressed his admiration for *Jerusalem* and I would urge you to see one or both of his renditions of the song on YouTube along with the more famous renditions by artists like Billy Bragg.

On YouTube, you can also see a version of the song sung by the group called Blake, whose name was inspired by the poet, and I am grateful to Alex Hopkirk of Infinite Artist Management for his explanation of how they came up with the name.

I have often visited Glastonbury Abbey in the course of my work as a tourist guide and the staff there have been unfailingly polite and professional in providing me with information and assistance. They have never pretended that King Arthur is really buried there but realise as well as anyone that the legend is sometimes as important as reality and that it is sometimes necessary to "print the legend", as the newspaper editor puts it in the final line of John Ford's film *The Man Who Shot Liberty Valance*.

David Boyle was most helpful in providing me with information about, amongst other things, how Stewart Headlam's championing of Blake led to the poet Robert Bridges suggesting to his friend Hubert Parry that he set *Jerusalem* to music in 1916.

I learned a great deal about the early days of the Women's Institute (about which I knew very little) with help from Fiona Hughes and the WI archivist Anne Stampfer.

During the course of my work in tourism, I have overheard (and stolen) many anecdotes. I am, in particular, grateful to my colleagues Ruth Polling for information on war memorials and to my friend Andrew Lumsden for information on the LaBouchere amendment which did so much to make life a misery for gay men after its passage into law in 1885.

Most of this book was written in Sussex during lockdown and I am grateful to the staff at Littlehampton Public Library and Rustington Museum for information and books providing useful background on the lives of the three men who helped to make *Jerusalem* England's second national anthem – Blake, Parry and Elgar.

I am also grateful to the support and tolerance of Leena Hazeldine, who shares a home with me in Sussex, and noticed – but never complained – when I once again opened my computer to start writing.

Introduction

In a house full of books one takes pride of place. It is a copy of *Paradise Lost*, John Milton's attempt to "justify the ways of God to men", which was left to me by my late father. What makes the book special is that the illustrations are by William Blake, who revered Milton and wrote a long poem about him, only one part of which is familiar today – the sixteen lines beginning "And did those feet in ancient time". It is one of our best known and most loved songs, often sung at festivals and even funerals.

We sang it at the funeral of a family friend recently and, although the words were in the service sheet, I realised that most of us did not need them, so familiar were they to us all. *Jerusalem*, as it is usually known, is also sung by the audience at the Last Night of the Proms and has become a kind of unofficial national anthem for England, used by all political parties to confirm both their patriotism and their idealism. It is also sung at sporting occasions and Danny Boyle used it in the opening ceremony for the London Olympics in 2012. As the ties that bind the countries of the United Kingdom together are loosened, there is a real possibility that it may become an official anthem for its most populous nation, although those who support our link with the royal family may have something to say about that.

And what an anthem it is! Most national songs consist of celebrations of the might and majesty of the country concerned: think of *Deutschland Uber Alles* or *Advance Australia Fair*. *Jerusalem*, however, asks questions. There are four in all, although there are only two actual question marks in the official text. Instead of bigging up England, which was not his style, Blake wonders if the son of God came to our shores two thousand years ago and resolves to help create a world worthy of him in the England of his day.

This was, in one of the poem's most famous phrases, a

country of "dark satanic mills" in the middle of an Industrial Revolution that would help to build up Britain's wealth and lead it to the kind of dominion over so much of the rest of the world which Blake would have hated. He was no imperialist but an opponent of slavery and a supporter of both the French and American revolutions. He was a patriot but not one who thought that it was his country's role to conquer and dominate others, rather to set an example. In fact, his opposition to purely patriotic wars led him into an argument with a soldier in the village of Felpham in Sussex where he had written the words to *Jerusalem*. Soon afterwards he returned to London with his wife Catherine. Truly, he was more at home amongst the satanic mills than he was in the green and pleasant land which he celebrated in the poem's other famous phrase.

Just over a century after the Blakes returned to London, Britain was again in the middle of a long war in Europe. In 1916, the poet laureate of the day, a largely forgotten figure called Robert Bridges, asked the composer Hubert Parry to set Blake's poem to music. Bridges felt that this would boost the morale of the people at a time of seemingly unending slaughter when nearly a million young men were cut down as they obediently climbed out of the trenches and attacked the unforgiving machine guns of the German army. An organisation called "Fight for Right" had been formed to support the war effort and the elderly Parry, who revered the German people and the string of famous composers who had come from amongst them, did his patriotic duty, despite his misgivings about the jingoistic nature of the movement his song was supporting.

One of the million who already died was the eighteen-year-old Jack Kipling, the only son of Rudyard Kipling, another writer who lived in Sussex. His house Bateman's is now owned by the National Trust which admits a steady stream of visitors, many of them attracted by their love of Kipling's famous stiff upper lip poem *If*. While neither Blake nor Parry felt enthusiasm for the wars being fought in Europe, Kipling was a keen patriot and encouraged, even facilitated, the enlistment of his only son by pulling strings to gain him a commission in the Irish Guards. As the luxurious house the Kiplings lived in and the Rolls Royce parked in the garage indicate, Rudyard could pull powerful strings and Jack was granted a commission despite suffering from the poor eyesight which also afflicted his father. Like other junior officers, who suffered the highest rate of casualties in the war, he was expected to lead his men into battle and he died at the Battle of Loos, where he first came under enemy fire, soon after arriving at the front in 1915. His body was buried in a grave which was not discovered until years later, despite the strenuous but unsuccessful efforts of his parents to locate it.[1]

Neither Blake nor Parry would have wished their work to be used to encourage young men like Jack Kipling to go to war and sacrifice their lives. Blake was a complicated man who lived in a world of his own but he knew enough about current affairs to question the automatic patriotism expected of most people in times of war. Parry too hated jingoism and became increasingly disillusioned at the use of his song by the kind of people who handed out white feathers to men who did not ostentatiously wear a military uniform in public.

As if to make up for his contribution to the war effort, Parry agreed that the Women's Suffrage movement could use the song as an anthem of their own. He lived just long enough to see women being granted a limited right to vote in early 1918 but died shortly before the First World War ended with the signing of the armistice in November that year. When women were given full equality in the franchise ten years later in 1928, Parry and Blake's song was adopted by the Women's Institute as their anthem. In the 1950s, it was sung at the Last Night of the Proms after Sir Malcolm Sargent introduced it as a staple of the programme.

A phrase from the poem was taken up by Hollywood to

provide the title for another example of sporting triumphs celebrated in the Oscar-winning film *Chariots of Fire*. This is the story of an English Jew, Harold Abrahams, and the devout Scottish Presbyterian, Eric Liddell, both of whom overcame personal battles to triumph at the Paris Olympics of 1924. Liddell, known as "the flying Scot", seemed to have lost his chance of a medal by refusing to run in the heats for the hundred metre race on a Sunday and thus had to miss out on the final. However, he won gold in the four hundred metre race, one he had never competed in before. Abrahams overcame the anti-Semitism directed towards him and the racism directed at his Turkish coach Sam Mussabini to win gold in the hundred metre race that Liddell had dropped out of. The film's scriptwriter Colin Welland heard the song one day and decided that the phrase chariots of fire would make a good title for their story. He famously told the Academy, when he accepted his Oscar for Best Original Screenplay that "the British are coming!"

They never arrived – in any numbers at least, but the song was to reappear in a popular film based, like *Chariots of Fire*, on a true story. *Calendar Girls* tells of a group of middle-aged women from Yorkshire who meet through their local Women's Institute and decide to raise money for a cancer ward after the husband of one of them succumbs to the disease. They do so by posing in various states of undress, removing their clothing while partially concealing their nudity by covering parts of their anatomy with strategically placed items associated with their role as makers of jam and cakes and servers of afternoon tea. It is through this film which, like *Chariots of Fire*, was later successfully adapted for the stage that many people today know the song which had its origins in Sussex 200 years ago.

Beginning with an eccentric artist, poet and visionary in Sussex, going on to a respectable composer and then a group of middle-aged women in Yorkshire, this is the story of England's most famous song.

Notes

1. The story of Jack Kipling is told in David Haig's play *My Boy Jack*. In the BBC television adaptation, Haig portrays Rudyard Kipling and Daniel Radcliffe plays Jack.

Chapter 1

Painter and Poet

It began with a poem. No one is sure exactly where William Blake wrote the sixteen lines which make up the words of what we now call *Jerusalem*, although Blake never called it that. For this socially awkward man, who was probably on what we would now call the autism spectrum, *Jerusalem* was a much longer poem subtitled *Emanations of the Giant Albion*. The shorter *Jerusalem* was written as an introduction to another of Blake's long poems called *Milton* in which he expresses his reverence for John Milton, that other pious and prickly English writer of poetry.

It was probably in the West Sussex village of Felpham that Blake wrote the famous lines wondering whether Christ came to England and in which he promises to build a new Jerusalem "in England's green and pleasant land". Other famous phrases from the poem – which only became a song much later in its existence – refer to "these dark satanic mills" and, in words picked up from the Bible itself, the famous "chariot of fire", a phrase recycled by Colin Welland when he wrote the script for the Oscar-winning film *Chariots of Fire*.

I often wonder what William Blake would have thought of so many people singing the words which he wrote over two hundred years ago. Thousands do so every year – at weddings, funerals, party political conferences, sporting events, at the Last Night of the Proms and whenever and wherever the Women's Institute meet. You can see multiple versions by different singers and groups singing *Jerusalem* on YouTube – Billy Bragg, Katherine Jenkins, The Fall, Emerson, Lake and Palmer and five thousand members of the Women's Institute singing to the Queen at the Albert Hall. You can see it used at the opening ceremony of the London Olympics of 2012, an event at which the dark satanic mills were given as much prominence as the green and pleasant land. Or you can watch a group of former public schoolboys who call themselves Blake singing it, the name of the band chosen to honour the writer of the words of the song.

Yet William Blake was much more than a poet. If asked to state his profession, he would probably have said that he was an engraver, possibly an artist. Although he wrote one of the most famous poems in the English language, he never made much of a living from his poetry. In fact, financially Blake was something of a failure. He and his wife lived in ten different homes, none of which they owned, and were often on the breadline.

Today Blake is lionised by the people of England and exhibitions of his art attract huge crowds. In 2019, the Tate Gallery – now rather clunkily renamed Tate Britain to distinguish it from Tate Modern, its hip sister museum further down the Thames – held an exhibition dedicated to Blake and a quarter of a million people paid their ten pounds to see his work.

They were not exactly queuing up to pay to see it when Blake was alive. The 2019 Tate exhibition included a recreation of the one-man show he held above his brother's shop in Soho in 1809. Hardly anybody came, Blake did not sell any paintings and the only review was scathing and dismissive. This review was written for a long-defunct magazine called *The Examiner* by James Hunt, brother of the more famous Leigh Hunt, who had founded the magazine together in a bid to make some money. (Leigh Hunt was a notorious sponger and was mercilessly satirised by Charles Dickens as Harold Skimpole in *Bleak House*.) James Hunt rubbished Blake's work and described him as "an unfortunate lunatic, whose personal inoffensiveness secures him from confinement". He goes on to describe the catalogue that Blake had produced for the exhibition as "a farrago of nonsense, unintelligibleness and egregious vanity, the wild effusions of a distempered brain".[1] A review like that severely tests the idea that there is no such thing as bad publicity and it is hard to imagine anyone being tempted to come and see Blake's work after they had read Hunt's opinion of it.

History, however, has long forgotten Hunt, who is chiefly remembered for his dismissal of Blake, while the subject of his scorn is now regarded as a true British hero. In contrast to Hunt, the contemporary art critic Jonathan Jones regards Blake as "the only artist we have ever produced who really captures the national genius" and says the illustration for his *Marriage of Heaven and Hell* are "like a fire of free thought blazing on the paper".[2] According to Jones, Blake's genius arose from the fact that he was both a poet and a painter. Britain may not have produced many great visual artists but the English language is "our greatest cultural achievement".

So it would be a mistake to climb into a time machine and go back to the nineteenth century and ask Blake whether he was a poet first and a painter second – or the other way around. The two were inextricably entwined for him and it was natural for Blake to illustrate his poems with engravings – or to adorn his engravings with poetry. Probably the most famous of his collections of poems, to which he painstakingly and skilfully added his own engravings, is *Songs of Innocence and Experience*. He sold only about thirty copies of *Songs* during his own lifetime but you can now purchase versions with mass-produced reproductions of Blake's pictures at prices Blake himself could only dream about.

Not much of a success in material terms – which would not have worried him overmuch – Blake was nevertheless a hard worker and a thorough professional in his craft of engraving. He had been born at 8 Broad (now Broadwick) Street in Soho, central London on 28 November 1757, the third of seven children. His father James worked in what we now often refer to as the rag trade, an important and reasonably profitable business before the days of mass production at a time when virtually all clothes were made by hand for the individual who would wear them.

Like many of those involved in trade, the Blakes were a dissenting family who worshipped God at their chapel. Nevertheless, James Blake knew that it was important to honour certain conventions and had William baptised at the nearby Saint James's church in Piccadilly, a stronghold of the established Church of England in the west end of London with a strong musical tradition. (*Jerusalem* has surely been sung there many times.) Saint James's is the only parish church outside the City of London designed by Christopher Wren. The steeple he designed is clearly observable along Piccadilly, although it is made from plastic, Wren's original having been destroyed by a German bomb during the blitz in 1940.

Blake only remained at school until the age of ten but he learned to read and write while there and was given a half-decent start in a life that was expected to be dominated by work. There are similarities in the backgrounds of William Blake and his near-contemporary, the Scottish poet, Robert Burns. As all Scots know, Burns was born in a "butt and ben" house in Alloway, now a suburb of the town of Ayr, on 25 January 1759 just over a year after Blake. He was the son of a tenant farmer and, although money was not plentiful in either household, both Burns' and Blake's fathers were able to provide their sons with a decent rudimentary education that made them aspire to more than mere survival in adulthood. Both writers later provided their countrymen with words and phrases which have been repeated ever since. While Blake celebrated England's green and pleasant land, the more down to earth Burns reflected that "the best laid plans of mice and men gang aft agley" (often go awry) after his ploughshare turned over the home of a field mouse.[3]

Both Blake and Burns were born in the days before universal state-provided education and had to rely on the devotion of parents who were both willing and able to pay for a decent rudimentary schooling for their sons. In 1772, Blake's parents paid fifty-two and a half pounds (the equivalent of nearly £5,000 today) to apprentice William with the engraver James Basire over the following seven years. He now began learning techniques that he would use throughout the rest of his life. Although they might today be considered little above the level of slavery, apprenticeships were for centuries considered a gateway into a professional life for (almost always) young men who were prepared to work hard and learn a trade which they would follow into adulthood. They might hope to take over from the master one day and possibly even marry his daughter before passing on the skills they had learned to the next generation. For centuries they would join a livery company or guild which would supervise their business, setting standards which they would be expected to maintain if they wanted to remain a member of the company, essential if they hoped to remain in business.

While apprenticed to Basire, Blake was sent to Westminster Abbey to draw the effigies and monuments there as part of a larger work his master had been commissioned to undertake. Today these monuments are mostly monochrome in appearance, various shades of grey interspersed with a few grand tombs of mostly forgotten figures retaining their brightly coloured paintwork. In Blake's time, more of them were painted, although the colours would be fading. We can imagine the young Blake lost in a world of his own in the Abbey, occasionally interrupted by loutish boys from the nearby Westminster School taunting this odd character who came to draw inside England's coronation church. Tormented by these scornful boys of his own age, Blake knocked one of them off a piece of scaffolding and complained to the Dean of the Abbey who, somewhat surprisingly, sided with him and not his privileged tormentors who were told to leave him alone to draw.

What was Blake's relationship with his master Basire like? Blake's biographer Peter Ackroyd noted that Basire's name was included in a list of "adversaries" by Blake but that he later crossed it out. It is not hard to think of the talented and individualistic young student champing at a bit he had been fastened into by the older, more conservative and hidebound teacher. At first he condemns the master but then his better nature reminds him that he is indebted to the man who taught him techniques that he could use for the rest of his life. There is something reassuring about this conflict between Blake's ambition and his gratitude, with an obligation to gratitude winning out in the end over his impatience.[4]

No such forgiveness was extended to Blake's next teacher, the well-known artist Sir Joshua Reynolds, who taught him at the Royal Academy, still situated on the north side of Piccadilly almost opposite the church where Blake had been baptised two decades earlier. Reynolds was, like most of his contemporaries, a portraitist who painted in oils and employed a style that strived to show the spirit of the person being portrayed without achieving a photographic likeness of him or (almost as often) her. He was influenced by the Flemish artist Peter Paul Rubens, who had painted the ceilings on the nearby Banqueting House in Whitehall which portrayed the early Stuart monarchs ascending to Heaven, emphasising the connection beyond God and King. This link had been broken by the Civil War, after which England had shown that it could manage perfectly well without a monarchy, thank you. When they returned after eleven years of joyless republicanism, the later Stuarts accepted the need to eat a humbler pie than they had previously been used to.

Blake had little time for Reynolds' ideas on what the teacher called "general beauty" and heartily despised the older artist. Time and again in his life, Blake would reject the accepted wisdom of the day and go his own way. Tact and respect for his elders were not part of his make-up and he was not slow to argue when he felt that he was in the right – which was most of the time. The loose brush strokes of oil painting were not for

Blake, who had trained as an engraver and who painstakingly worked the copper plates which he used to illustrate poems that he and other writers produced. In doing so he would cut into the plates with a type of knife known as a burin. This technique did not allow for the loose impressionistic style that Reynolds and his contemporaries adopted and from which they earned a decent living, mainly by painting portraits.

This was a better living than Blake could ever earn and that may have contributed to his contempt for and conflict with the norms of the day. Blake had no interest in becoming a fashionable portraitist for high-born and wealthy customers in eighteenth century England. He was looking further back to the classical world and to the renaissance in which the ancient world was reborn through the works of men like Michelangelo and Leonardo.

Blake was used to hard work from an early age but had little interest in accumulating money or achieving high status. In a poignant remark, for which she is probably best remembered, Blake's long-suffering wife Catherine said, "I have very little of Mister Blake's company: he is always in Paradise."[5] However often he ambled off to Paradise, Catherine was devoted to William. He had taught her to read and write, her signature on the marriage certificate being simply a cross. In this, she resembles Anne Hathaway, another famous author's wife, although there is no good evidence that William Shakespeare ever led her out of the illiteracy which was standard for women in Tudor England. Catherine helped her husband in his work and was always by his side. There are stories that he wanted to bring another woman into their relationship but nothing ever came of this and William's sensual desires had to be satisfied within his marriage to Catherine. They would sometimes sit naked in their garden reading *Paradise Lost* together and, when Blake's friend and business partner Thomas Butts arrived one day to find them there in a state of undress, he was invited in to join them, Willian cheerfully saying, "It's only Adam and Eve, you know."[6] However their relationship progressed, the marriage remained devoted but childless and the two are buried together at Bunhill Fields in London.

It would not be quite true to say that Blake was completely ignored by his contemporaries but, while he was alive, he knew nothing like the level of success and affection in which he is held today. If they regarded him at all, most people in Victorian Britain looked on him as a harmless lunatic. His contemporary William Wordsworth had transcribed some of Blake's poems, such as the famous *Tyger*, but thought him mad, as did Robert Southey, brother-in-law of Wordsworth's fellow poet Samuel Taylor Coleridge, who called him "a decided madman". In his later years, Blake was able to compensate slightly for the failure of his solo exhibition by gaining a group of admirers who revered him. These were The Ancients, who were based in the Kent village of Shoreham, where its most famous member, the painter Samuel Palmer, lived. The Ancients would meet at Blake's last home in Fountain Court near the Strand, roughly where the Savoy Hotel now stands. They became a kind of early version of the Pre-Raphaelite Brotherhood, rejecting conventional paths to artistic success as they looked back to an ideal older world.

Another man associated with William Blake is Thomas Paine, who popularised the phrase "common sense" and published a pamphlet of that name, which is still in print. Like Blake, Paine lived for a time in Sussex and even has a type of beer produced there named after him.[7] It was in Sussex that Paine came to political maturity and developed ideas that led him to France and, later, America, where he supported the revolutions led by the people of both countries to throw off the shackles of monarchy, their own in the case of the French and that of George III of Britain in the case of the Americans, who were encouraged in their attempts to set up a republic by Paine.

Tom Paine almost did not make it to America and narrowly escaped becoming one of the children devoured by the revolution, as the French King Louis XVI called those who had supported the Revolution but fell victim to the guillotine. Paine had been marked for execution along with Robespierre and a cross was marked on the door of his cell to indicate his fate. Luckily for him, the cross was daubed on the inside of the door, which was often left open for visitors but was closed when they came to collect customers for beheading. This – literally – saved the neck of a man who had supported the French desire for freedom but was considered unsound by the custodians of the new order. Paine was pragmatic enough not to point out this piece of carelessness on the part of his gaolers and promptly set off for America, where he also managed to fall out with the citizens of the new republic despite his enthusiastic support for their uprising against British rule.

Fortunately for him, Paine's disputes with his new countrymen, who were too God-fearing for his taste, did not prove fatal and he lived out the rest of his years in relative peace with his companion Marguerite and her sons. Only six people came to his funeral and his grave has been lost, although the site of his death in New York is identified by a memorial plaque. As with Blake, Paine had the gift of falling out with those he supported and it was not until long after his death that he was lionised by their descendants. While Blake spent his entire life in England, mostly in London, Paine lived in different parts of England, France and, finally, America. Death did not end his travels, however, as the radical writer William Cobbett brought his bones back to England, after which they were lost.

Blake's bones have also been subject to relocation, albeit by a much shorter distance. A Portuguese couple, Luis and Carol Garrido, spent several years conducting some rather morbid detective work to locate the exact spot where he was buried and, on 12 August 2018, a new gravestone was unveiled by the

Blake Society to mark this spot at Bunhill Fields near to those of other well-known non-conformist writers like John Bunyan and Daniel Defoe, who already had more imposing monuments erected in their honour.[8]

Did Paine and Blake ever meet in the flesh? The jury is out on that question. A popular legend has Blake warning Paine of his imminent arrest by the authorities, leading Paine to flee to France in early 1792. In his biography of Blake, however, Peter Ackroyd does not cover this story, even though Paine is mentioned several times. They moved in the same circles and had similar sympathies – the three r's of revolutionary, republican and radical – but they had different personalities and priorities. Paine was a political figure who supported the right of common people to decide how they should be governed. Blake was more interested in paradise than politics and a large part of his life was devoted to the world of the spirit. It is certainly possible that they met and shook hands but, given their different personalities and temperaments, it is quite possible that this meeting was little more than a "How do you do, Mister Blake/ Mister Paine" exchange of pleasantries.

They did meet, however, in the imagination of Jack Shepherd, an actor and playwright best known for portraying the lugubrious detective Wycliffe in the television series of that name. Shepherd has written over a dozen plays and his portrayal of an imagined meeting between the two radicals resulted in one called *In Lambeth*, which has been staged several times in London and once in Lewes, where Paine lived. In the play, Paine, pursued by an angry mob of anti-republicans, takes shelter in the Lambeth home of the Blakes where he finds William and Catherine reading *Paradise Lost* in their garden without any clothes on, as was their habit. The play was also broadcast on television with Mark Rylance portraying Blake and the late Bob Peck reprising his performance on stage as Tom Paine.

The Lambeth house where they supposedly met also

featured in another fictional story featuring Blake, *Burning Bright* by Tracey Chevalier, a novelist who often fictionalises stories of historical figures such as Mary Anning the fossil hunter in *Remarkable Creatures* and, most famously, the painter Johannes Vermeer and the unknown but imagined subject of the painting *Girl with a Pearl Earring*. In the novel, Chevalier, the title of whose book comes from the poem *Tyger* by Blake, shows us a man of great moral courage who befriends and assists the young Jemm Kellaway after he arrives in London from Dorset. A circus is featured in the story and this is historically accurate as Lambeth was where Philip Astley ran his circus in the late eighteenth and early nineteenth century. Astley demonstrated his horse-riding skills in a circular auditorium rather than in a straight line, thus giving a name to this popular attraction, the word circus deriving from the Latin word for circle.

The house in Hercules Road in Lambeth was named after the strong man who featured in Philip Astley's circus shows, as he owned the land on which it was built. It provides the setting for *In Lambeth* and is featured in the backdrop to Chevalier's novel, but has long since been demolished. All that remains of it is a housing estate named after Blake by the City of London Corporation, which now owns the land. It is the only London house the Blakes lived in which is south of the Thames and it is near the church where they married, St Mary's, Battersea. The Blakes spent a decade in Lambeth and seemed to have been happy there – if "happy" is a word that could ever be applied to a man like William Blake – but money problems and the chance to move to a rural home led them to relocate to Sussex in 1800.

It was William Hayley who offered the Blakes both a home in the Sussex village of Felpham and a steady source of income. Largely forgotten now, Hayley was a wealthy minor poet and also the friend of the better known and more frequently read William Cowper. The sculptor John Flaxman had encouraged Hayley to commission an engraving of his son, John Alphonso, from Blake. Despite his dissatisfaction with both the resulting work and Blake's slowness in completing it – it was not finished until after John Alphonso had died at the age of nineteen – Hayley took on Blake as a project. After the death of John, who had been born to his housekeeper rather than his wife, Hayley may have been looking for a substitute son and chose Blake, whom he described as his "secretary". Fortunately, this was not a word he used when talking to Blake, who would have bridled at performing a role that put him only slightly above the level of a servant.

It was typical of Blake to accept an offer from a well-meaning man of superior income but inferior talent and then to chafe under the restrictions imposed by being at the beck and call of a patron. Although he never made much money, Blake was a proud and independent man who had always made his own way in the world. In the epic poem that he called *Jerusalem*, a far longer one than the sixteen lines we often sing, Blake wrote:

I must create a system, or be enslav'd by another man's;
I will not reason and compare; my business is to create.[9]

The lines are uttered by Blake's mythical hero Los but they could equally apply to the poet himself. Blake was simply not cut out to be a second in command to Hayley – or anyone else – and creative freedom was always more important than commercial success.

At first, the move to Sussex from Lambeth had seemed a success. William and Catherine enjoyed living in their country cottage and he had a steady source of work from Hayley, who lived in a large house nearby. Their one attempt to make money, however, was not a success. They decided to bypass conventional publishing and produce their own book of ballads on animals, written by Hayley, illustrated by Blake and printed in nearby Chichester. Making drawings of animals was not Blake's strong point, however, and the book did not sell well. Neither man was a natural entrepreneur, Hayley being independently wealthy and Blake being simply too independent to trim his talents to the marketplace.

Sussex was to be important for Blake, however, because it was where the germ of *Jerusalem* came into being. It is impossible to tell exactly when an idea comes into a writer's mind unless that writer tells the world through his letters and/or diaries. No diaries exist for Blake and most of his letters were written mainly for business purposes. He was usually too busy with his engraving duties to write down his thoughts on what would have been expensive sheets of paper for a never wealthy couple. He seems to have had little interest in posterity, being more concerned with the journey to paradise after his death.

The writer David Boyle believes that Blake wrote the words of *Jerusalem* when he moved back to London and was living in South Molton Street.[10] However, the famous phrase "England's green and pleasant land" at least suggests Sussex as an inspiration, while many believe that the "dark satanic mills" were inspired by the Albion Flour Mills near the River Thames in London. The Albion Mills had been burnt down – possibly deliberately – in 1791, over a decade before *Jerusalem* was written, but they would have been familiar to Blake as a symbol of the increasing industrialisation in Britain at the time. The mills may also have represented the established Church of England, another symbol of oppression to him.

The poem we now refer to as *Jerusalem* first came into being at the start of a much longer, and for many people, virtually unreadable work called *Milton* in which the poet Blake imagines a journey Milton takes from Heaven back to earth to purge himself of his puritan attitudes. Milton arrives in Lambeth, where he enters Blake's body through his left foot. The scene then shifts to the Blakes' cottage in Felpham where a twelve-year-old girl called Ololon comes down to him via a skylark and ends up joining Milton's body in a non-sexual way.

The poem shifts from celestial spheres to contemporary England as Blake inserts a kind of tube map of London on top of an imagined world inhabited by real people like Milton and imagined characters such as Los and Palamabron. Safe to say, it is not an easy read and we are a long way from the Women's Institute and the Royal Albert Hall, through which most of us are familiar with the sixteen line poem by Blake which begins this epic work.

Blake was familiar with Milton's work and drew illustrations for *Paradise Lost*. He also inserted "To Justify the Ways of God to Men" above his preface of *Milton*, referencing Milton's reason for writing about the expulsion of Satan from Heaven and the subsequent fall of Adam and Eve. These two cantankerous and pious Englishmen had a good deal in common, although their lives took very different paths. Milton, a good linguist, was Secretary for Foreign Tongues under Oliver Cromwell and acted as a kind of propagandist for the short-lived republic he served with enthusiasm. He argued in favour of divorce and against monarchy but eventually retired from public life after Cromwell's death and the restoration of King Charles II. Without renouncing his previous views, he kept his head down and escaped punishment for supporting the republic, dedicating the later part of his life to writing *Paradise Lost* while his wife and daughters read Greek and Latin texts to the now blind poet without being able to understand a word of what they were saying.

This now seems an act of almost sadistic cruelty, but Milton probably regarded it as a kindness, believing that "one tongue is sufficient for a woman". He wrote moving sonnets about the death of his second wife as well as the loss of his sight but Milton was not familiar with the concept of sexism. He describes Adam and Eve enjoying conjugal love in *Paradise Lost*, but Eve's role is to serve Adam and she is the one who gets the blame for eating that apple and bringing about the Fall. The ending of this great epic poem, in which Adam and Eve depart from the Garden of Eden, is almost unbearably moving as this all-too human couple venture into the real world and leave Paradise behind. Whatever his talents, Blake could never write as movingly as this.

Both Blake and Milton lived in times of great upheaval. Milton saw – and was at the centre of – the transformation of Britain from a monarchy to a republic in the middle of the seventeenth century. He then had to witness the return of the monarchy when Cromwell's republic collapsed. Cromwell had called his government the Commonwealth, as the wealth was supposed to be shared around fairly. In practice, England was not ready for socialism and, deprived of their traditional pleasures by the puritans, the people eagerly welcomed Charles II back after Cromwell died. When he saw the crowds cheering his return, Charles remarked with cheerful cynicism that he would never have stayed away for so long had he known that his people had missed him so much.

Blake's time also saw a huge change in Britain. Not only had an industrial revolution produced those infamous dark satanic mills, but the French Revolution had led to a long war with a France which had not only dispensed with but effectively annihilated its monarchy. Blake's contemporary William Wordsworth had travelled to France, fallen in love and had a child with a Frenchwoman and had written in his autobiographical poem *The Prelude* the famous lines: "Bliss it was in that dawn to be alive, But to be young was very heaven." Unlike Blake, Wordsworth soon lost his youthful idealism and adopted the anti-French attitude of the British establishment once the guillotine started to do its gruesome work. When Napoleon took over in France, war with Britain became inevitable.

There is warfare in the words of *Jerusalem* but it was of a spiritual rather than a military kind. Blake, no lover of monarchy, supported the ideals behind the French Revolution and was hostile to the war Britain was fighting against France. You cannot take a poem (or any work of art) out of the context of where and when it was written. The Blakes were living in a Sussex village by the English Channel in the middle of a long war and at a time of social upheaval and massive industrialisation. *Jerusalem* might look both back to the idea that Jesus came to England and forward to the building of a new Jerusalem within these shores, but they are also infected with the spirit of the time when they are written.

Wherever Blake first wrote the words of *Jerusalem* down, we can safely say that they came into being either during or soon after his time in Felpham because the larger work *Milton* was dated to 1804, the year after the couple left the village. The Blakes had never lived outside London before the move to Sussex. Although they could stroll down to look at the sea from their cottage, Catherine seems to have found it increasingly damp and cold and may well have yearned for the bustle and crowds of London, which she had been used to for her whole life. After barely two years away, they decided to end their rural experiment and return to the city. Things came to a head when Blake had a public row with a soldier called John Scofield, who came into the poet's garden one day in the summer of 1803. Scofield (sometimes spelt Schofield) was doing some casual work there for the gardener but Blake disliked the idea of having a uniformed soldier in his home and told him to leave. Scofield took exception to this treatment and Blake forcibly marched his unwanted visitor back to the nearby Fox Inn where he was billeted. There is something comical about the pacific but hot-tempered poet and painter forcibly marching a professional fighting man off the premises and down the street while the soldier protests and fulminates. It was soon to turn serious, however.

Both men's later accounts of the incident vary widely, but Scofield was obviously angry at his treatment by this unsound and radical artist who had treated one of the nation's loyal soldiers with such disdain. Rather than cooling down afterwards, Scofield became determined to get even with Blake and, possibly egged on by his fellow soldiers and aware of the humiliation of being bested by a mere artist, he accused Blake of sedition, saying that he had "damned" the king and called his soldiers "slaves". This is entirely believable from Blake, who was not one to hide his opinions when his blood was up. Yet it was particularly unwise at a time of war with France when Britain was threatened with invasion from nearby France. Scofield made a deposition to the magistrates in Chichester and Blake had to stand trial and faced the real prospect of being imprisoned for expressing his views too forcibly.

In a letter to Thomas Butt, Blake realises that he may have overstepped the mark in arguing with Scofield and, although he defends his actions, and says that the accusation levelled against him is "Fabricated Perjury", he shows enough self-knowledge to pen a verse in the letter which recognises and even expresses regret for his headstrong nature:

O why was I born with a different face?
Why was I not born like the rest of my race?
When I look each one starts! when I speak I offend
Then I'm silent & passive & lose every Friend
Then my verse I dishonour. My pictures despise
My person degrade & my temper chastise
And the pen is my terror. the pencil my shame
All my Talents I bury, and Dead is my Fame
I am either too low or too highly priz'd
When Elate I am Envy'd, When Meek I'm despis'd.[11]

Blake was certainly not born like the rest of his race. He had a temper and could be foolhardy in expressing his views, but he was also terrified at the idea of imprisonment. No man would have been less suited to confinement than him, used as he was to working with Catherine at his side, seeing visions of his beloved dead brother Robert as well as angels and spirits. It is not hard to imagine how this unworldly man would have been treated by his fellow prisoners if he had been sent to gaol. Blake became anxious and nervous at the thought of losing his freedom and longed to return to London, where he felt more at home. He may have railed against them in his most famous poem but you feel that Blake's true home was next to the dark satanic mills, rather than in the green and pleasant land, where people tend to be conservative, suspicious of outsiders and conventionally patriotic.

It was at Blake's trial that Hayley came to the rescue. Not only did he put up the hundred pounds bail money (which Blake could never have afforded) but he found a lawyer, Samuel Rose, who did a good job of defending Blake by portraying him in the court as an upstanding patriot persecuted by an untrustworthy and vindictive soldier. Fortunately, Blake was not called upon to give evidence, when his fiery temper and radical sympathies would probably have been revealed, and with the soldiers who testified against him contradicting each other in their evidence, he was swiftly acquitted. While a uniform might win you the sympathy of a jury today, soldiers were often treated with suspicion two hundred years ago and had a reputation for opportunism and irresponsibility. They might look glamorous in scarlet and be needed to defend the country in times of war but they were not to be trusted in peacetime. Even the Duke of Wellington cheerfully described his own troops as "the scum of the earth".

Indeed, soldiers were not generally honoured in Britain with war memorials until after the First World War.[12] By then, soldiering had changed from being the profession of a corps of smart-looking but untrustworthy characters to the duty of young men who volunteered or were conscripted to fight for king and country. These soldiers were honoured by the singing of a song first written as a poem by Blake, a peace-loving man who narrowly escaped imprisonment after arguing with a soldier in the village where both men were based, one trying to earn a living, the other protecting the country from invasion.

But we must leave Blake now, as he and Catherine return to London, where they were to live for the rest of their lives, never far from poverty, to die in obscurity before he was brought back to public notice and the affection of the British people many years later. Our next stop is in Somerset, where the legend Blake gave voice to first came into being.

Notes

1. Quoted in the Tate Gallery guide to the Blake exhibition, 2019
2. From an article in the Guardian, 12 January 2010
3. *To a Louse* by Robert Burns. The phrase "of mice and men" was used by John Steinbeck as the title of his famous story about the struggles of George and Lennie, two itinerant farm workers brought down by forces more powerful than them.
4. *Blake* by Peter Ackroyd (page 51)
5. This often-quoted remark was made by Catherine Blake to Seymour Kirkup, a young friend of theirs whom they met in later life. (Ackroyd, page 295)
6. poetryfoundation.org/poets/william-blake
7. Tom Paine Ale, produced in Lewes by Harvey's. Be careful if you try it – it has an abv of 6.8%, which is at least fifty per cent stronger than most beers.
8. blakesociety.org/wp-content/uploads/2017/08/Blakes-Grave.pdf
9. *Jerusalem, Chapter One* (line 20 after plate 10)
10. David Boyle *Jerusalem* (ebook) introduction

11. erdman.blakearchive.org/#b15 (Blake's letter is reproduced on pages 731-3)
12. Thanks to Ruth Polling for the information on war memorials.

Chapter 2

Bare Ruined Choirs

Most guide books will tell you that Saint Martin's in Canterbury is the oldest parish church in these islands. It has been in continuous use since it was founded over fourteen centuries ago as a chapel for Queen Bertha, wife of King Ethelbert of Kent, who had agreed to allow his wife to continue practising her curious Christian faith when she came over from France to be married to him. Ethelbert later adopted Christianity after being baptised by Saint Augustine, who had himself been sent to England by Pope Gregory to convert the English. In one of history's earliest puns, Gregory had said that the fair-haired and blue-eyed English people he saw in the slave market in Rome were "non Angli, sed angeli" – "not Angles, but angels". Gregory's little joke works in both the original Latin and in modern English.

Christianity existed in England before Gregory sent Augustine to bring the Angles/angels back to the true faith in 597 AD. One of England's most famous saints, Cuthbert, lived in the north of what is now a distinct nation but was then divided into separate (and often-warring) kingdoms. Paganism was still strong here as Augustine's follower Paulinus was sent to bring Christianity northwards from Canterbury. Paulinus was to become the first Archbishop of York, while Augustine was the first Archbishop of Canterbury and head of the church of England, then still firmly under the control of Rome. Canterbury and York remain the seats of the Church of England's two archbishoprics and, although it is not unknown for men (always men – so far, at least) to move from one to the other, an old rivalry between these two Christian cathedrals remains. Canterbury Cathedral may be older but York Minster, as the locals like to remind visitors, York's cathedral is the largest medieval church in the country. (Liverpool's is larger but is a modern building.)

A similar tension existed between the original Christian church in England and the one that arrived with Augustine. It was not until the year 664 that the old Celtic Christianity and the new Roman version came together at the Synod of Whitby and agreed to amalgamate. The Romans were masters now and almost all of their customs, such as calculating the date of Easter and the type of tonsures worn by the monks, were adopted by the new unified church. It would take almost another thousand years for English Christians to re-establish autonomy from Rome when the Church of England was established. This was almost a century after Martin Luther had supposedly nailed his ninety-five theses attacking corruption in the Catholic church to the door of All Saints Church in Wittenberg. Ninety-five theses is a lot: Luther had plenty of complaints and the list of them was probably too long to fit onto a single sheet of paper attachable to a church door. However, they were sent to the Archbishop of Mainz, who was lining the coffers of the church with the money people paid to speed their way through Purgatory in order to arrive in Heaven more quickly. Whether Luther's theses were nailed to a church door or not, the Reformation had begun. It took the best part of another century, but this led to the establishment of an independent and Protestant Church of England, one which still owns and maintains the abbey where, according to legend, a church much older than St Martin's in Canterbury was built.

This first church was supposedly built in Glastonbury in Somerset. Now probably more famous for the annual music festival which takes place on Michael Eavis's farm five miles away, Glastonbury is a smallish town of around ten thousand souls which is home to a once huge monastery. This is now a romantic ruin with the bare ruined choirs immortalised in Shakespeare's sonnet seventy-three, in which the poet mourns the dying embers of his relationship with an unknown patron.

He compares it to those ruined choirs, which Shakespeare would have remembered from his youth as he grew up during the reign of Elizabeth I in the aftermath of the dissolution of the monasteries when Elizabeth's father Henry VIII had fallen out with the pope and established an independent – later Protestant – Church of England. Henry, by the way, had little time for Luther's ideas and considered himself a good Catholic to the end of his life, just one not subservient to the pope.

Long before its adherents began fighting each other over who was the real head of the church, pope or king, Christians had been a persecuted but unified sect. One of the early adherents of Christianity was Joseph of Arimathea, who had been present a the crucifixion and had helped to bury Jesus afterwards. In some versions of the story, he is related to Christ, being an uncle of the Virgin Mary. Our English legend has Joseph coming here as a missionary and trader, specifically a tin merchant, doing business and spreading the faith, just as William Blake did many centuries later. Arriving in Glastonbury and feeling weary after a long day's travelling he rested by Wirral (weary-all) Hill and placed his staff in the ground. The staff took root overnight and, taking this as a sign from God that he should build a church there, he constructed a small and simple place of worship which later grew into Glastonbury Abbey. Joseph's staff grew into a thorn tree which flowers twice a year at Christmas and Easter, a Christmas blossom sent to the sovereign every year as a gift.

This gift might have been considered necessary in order to keep the monarch on the abbey's side. Glastonbury Abbey was laid waste by the officers of King Henry VIII when he broke with Rome, not for some high point of principle but because the pope had refused to grant him a divorce from his first wife Catherine of Aragon. Under normal circumstances the king might well have obtained his divorce but, as Pope Clement VII was pretty much under the thumb of Holy Roman Emperor Charles V, who was the nephew of Catherine of Aragon, there was little chance that this would happen. The Aragons were certainly not going to have Catherine and their ancient name humiliated by some jumped up English monarch whose grandfather had been merely an obscure Welsh squire.

As a result of the break with Rome, Henry VIII simply denied the authority of the pope in England and shunted Catherine aside, divorcing her so he could marry his mistress Anne Boleyn, hoping that she would provide him with a son to whom he could pass the crown. The hope proved vain, their daughter Elizabeth arrived but a son was stillborn and Anne went to the Tower where she was executed, despite her hope for a last minute act of clemency from the man who had once doted on her.

Amongst the collateral damage of the break with Rome were men like Thomas Wolsey, who had failed to negotiate the divorce that Henry wanted, and Thomas More who refused to accept the king's authority over the pope in doctrinal matters. A less well-known victim was Richard Whiting, the Abbot of Glastonbury, a man in his late seventies who had signed the Act of Supremacy recognising the monarch as head of the Church of England but found that this was not enough to save either him or his abbey. He and two other monks were dragged to the top of Glastonbury Tor where they were hung, drawn and quartered, the remains of their corpses displayed around the county so that no one would be in any doubt as to what would happen to anyone who stayed loyal to the pope rather than the king. The man who masterminded the dissolution of the monasteries was Henry's chief gofer, Thomas Cromwell, who looted the abbey of its wealth, leaving only those bare ruined choirs.

There are, however, enough ruined choirs left standing in Glastonbury Abbey to justify the charging of an entrance fee to view them. Costumed guides bring the story of the church, its monks and pilgrims to life and the more adventurous and fit visitor can walk up the nearby Glastonbury Tor to survey the surrounding low-lying countryside from the thirteenth century church tower of Saint Michael, where Whiting had been so brutally executed in 1539. Whiting had been interrogated at the Tower of London by Thomas Cromwell, who found later what it was like to incur the displeasure of the king when he too was imprisoned there and executed near where Thomas More had earlier felt the axe's edge. More, like Whiting, has been beatified by the Catholic church and is now Saint rather than Sir Thomas. Unsurprisingly, no such honour was extended to Cromwell, who would have to be content with providing Hilary Mantel with subject matter for her trilogy of acclaimed novels.

Stand on top of Glastonbury Tor looking westwards towards Taunton and Bridgewater and look out over the flat land of what was once a very marshy landscape, since drained to provide fertile land for farms and vineyards which produce bottles of English wine for our dinner tables. It is just a small leap of imagination to picture this low-lying land covered in water. Archaeologists have found evidence that a great tsunami, which claimed thousands of lives, burst from the River Severn in January 1607 to flood the area.[1] If we can see the Somerset Levels as a once huge inland sea, could we also imagine Morgan le Fay bringing the body of her dying half-brother King Arthur to his final resting place on the Isle of Avalon down below the Tor in the ruined abbey? Marion Zimmer Bradley imagined just such a scene in her version of the Arthurian legend *The Mists of Avalon* and the site obviously meant much to her, as her ashes were scattered from the top of the Tor after she died in 1999. John Boorman's film version of the story *Excalibur* also has Arthur brought over the sea for burial just before the final credits roll.

King Arthur and the Knights of the Round Table are known throughout the English-speaking world and most visitors to Glastonbury will want to take a photograph of the supposed site of Arthur's grave in the abbey ruins. However, if the legend of Joseph of Arimathea founding a church that grew into Glastonbury Abbey is thin, the discovery of King Arthur's grave there in 1191 is positively anorexic in comparison, an example of medieval opportunism combined with wishful thinking. It came about after another King Henry had fallen out with an earlier Thomas three hundred years before Henry VIII had Thomas More executed.

The first of the Plantagenet kings, Henry II, argued with his former friend Thomas a Becket who, despite never have been ordained as a priest, was appointed as Archbishop of Canterbury by the king, specifically to help in the reform of church laws. Becket, however, turned from Henry and actually hampered his attempts to control the church until he was killed at Canterbury Cathedral in 1179 by a group of knights who took the king at his word when he cried out in frustration, "Will no one rid me of this low born, troublesome priest?" After this shocking act of violence in a house of God against the head of the church, Henry was made to do penance and this proud king was flogged by monks and forced to admit his faults.

A less well-known aspect of the Becket story is the effect it had on the medieval tourist industry. In the Middle Ages, people rarely travelled and many would never venture far away from the town or village where they were born. Those who did would usually visit a holy site, often in company with others, sometimes in the hope that their illnesses and disabilities might be cured and/or their sins forgiven through proximity to a saint or other holy figure. The abbey at Glastonbury was a natural destination for them and, in the days before satnav and decent maps, it was quite easy to see the nearby Tor from a distance as you came over the Mendip Hills. Both the abbey and the nearby businesses would benefit from the presence of people needing the three staple requirements of the tourist – food, shelter and souvenirs. People often loosen their purse strings when away from home and many of these businesses would be used to benefiting from the generosity of travellers who hoped that proximity to a holy place would improve their health, both physically and spiritually.

After the martyrdom of Becket, Glastonbury fell out of favour and Canterbury became the go-to place for those seeking the benefits – and fun – to be had from a pilgrimage. It even affected our language, the gentle trot on horseback to this fashionable new destination becoming known as a "canter", a common term used by riders to this day. William Blake even made a series of etchings depicting the pilgrims who accompanied Geoffrey Chaucer and told tales on the road to Canterbury. Unsurprisingly, he fell out with William Stodhard, who had first proposed the project but who ended up choosing another artist to fulfil it.

What were the merchants and monks of Glastonbury to do now that people were heading east to Kent rather than west to Somerset? How could they persuade them to travel in the opposite direction? The abbey itself had suffered from a big fire in 1184 and was badly in need of funds for repairs. How could they be raised? And how could King Henry stop people banging on about that low-born troublesome former friend who had turned against him and caused so much trouble? They needed a big name and came up with the biggest of all, an English hero who had stood out against a foreign invader and gone down in history – or at least in legend, there being little difference between the two in the Middle Ages.

They needed King Arthur.

And so they found him. According to *De Principis Instructione* by Gerald of Wales, the tomb of Arthur and Guinevere was discovered in the year 1191, just over two decades after Becket had been murdered at Canterbury by Henry's over-enthusiastic knights. That may seem like a long gap in our internet-led world, but news travelled more slowly in medieval times. Geoffrey of Monmouth had published a *History of the Kings of Britain* in 1138 and this included the story of Arthur and Guinevere, so it was fresh in the minds of the people of England, who had never completely forgotten the ancient warrior who fought against his own incestuously conceived son Mordred.

Both Geoffrey of Monmouth, who was a monk, and Gerald, who was a civil servant in the court of King Henry, had strong Welsh connections. So too did Arthur and his enabler Merlin, who was largely a creation of Geoffrey. But why was Arthur's tomb discovered in Glastonbury, apart from the need for the abbey to dig up a lucrative new attraction which could persuade pilgrims to return there instead of going off to nouveau riche Canterbury?

The answer lies in the Holy Grail, the item which links King Arthur to Joseph of Arimathea. We now use the phrase "holy grail" to signify anything unobtainable or elusive but it derives from a specific item, a vessel that Jesus drank from at the Last Supper and was later used by Joseph of Arimathea to gather Christ's blood as he was being crucified. Arthur's knights went searching for this Holy Grail, which had been buried by Joseph around the time he built our first church, the one which later grew into Glastonbury Abbey and is now mainly the bare ruined choirs with a gift shop and museum close at hand.

We talk about fake news as if it is something new but it is really just a new phrase for an old phenomenon. From the legend of Robin Hood to the tale of Lady Godiva – both historical figures hopelessly obscured by the myths which surround them – it has been hard to separate fact from fiction when you go back a few centuries, let alone a thousand years or more. Arthur, if he existed at all, lived at a time known as the dark ages, which gives you an idea of how obscure it was, while Joseph of Arimathea was contemporary with Christ himself.

Nevertheless, the abbey at Glastonbury needed a draw and one was conveniently found in the grave of King Arthur when it was unearthed in 1191. Gerald of Wales describes how:

The body of King Arthur ... was found in our own days at Glastonbury, deep down in the earth and encoffined in a hollow oak between two stone pyramid s ... two parts of the tomb, to wit, the head, were allotted to the bones of the man, while the remaining third ... contained the bones of a woman ... there was found a yellow tress of woman's hair still retaining its colour and freshness; but when a certain monk snatched it and lifted it with greedy hand, it straightaway all of it fell into dust ... the bones of Arthur ... were so huge that his shank-bone when placed against the tallest man in the place, reached a good three inches above his knee ... the eye-socket was a good palm in width ... there were ten wounds or more, all of which were scarred over, save one larger than the rest, which had made a great hole.[2]

So, the skeleton was that of a fighter as his bones were marked with "ten wounds or more". He was big and a woman (presumably his wife) was buried next to him. You can almost hear Gerald and the monks thinking and then saying – this will do for Arthur.

To be fair to Glastonbury Abbey, they do not try to pretend that the grave of King Arthur was a genuine find. On their website, the story of Arthur is classified under the category "Myths and Legends" next to that of Joseph of Arimathea and they openly admit that: "Very little reliable evidence survives from the fifth and sixth centuries when the historical Arthur lived."[3]

If you visit the abbey today you see the supposed grave of King Arthur soon after you enter. Nearby is a large cross given by the Queen which tactfully – and accurately – says that "it marks a Christian sanctuary so ancient that only legend can record its origin". Most people who visit simply want a photograph of "King Arthur's Grave" without bothering overmuch about the historical accuracy of the sign they are taking a picture of.

The sign by Arthur's grave also says that his body and that of

Guinevere (or whoever's bones they discovered) was moved into a black marble tomb in 1278, nearly a century after they were first discovered. This was done in the presence of King Edward I, a notably warlike medieval monarch who was keen to give his killing of people from other countries (particularly Scotland) a degree of respectability by allying himself with the image of Arthur. Like most modern tourists, Edward would not have been concerned overmuch with historical facts when he was fighting wars and conducting the medieval equivalent of ethnic cleansing. All of the fairly dubious evidence of a genuine grave for King Arthur disappeared at the time of the reformation so what we see now is simply a sign that his grave was discovered "here", later moved to "there" and then destroyed when church and king clashed three and a half centuries after it was uncovered and two and a half after it was moved.

This is pretty thin stuff for a modern archaeologist, who will tell you that it is easy when digging down into the past to put two and two together to make five. The tendency to exaggerate the value and importance of your finds is irresistible for many diggers. It is one which the famous nineteenth century German businessman and archaeologist Heinrich Schliemann was unable to resist. After he decided that he had discovered the ancient city of Troy at Hissarlik in Turkey, he started digging enthusiastically, using techniques that would lead to him being immediately thrown out of and permanently banned from any excavation conducted today. Nevertheless, he uncovered some ancient gold stores, which he immediately defined as "Priam's treasure", and even dressed his young wife Sophia in what he said, with forgivably romantic exaggeration, were the "jewels of Helen of Troy".

Archaeologists today take the attitude that nothing can be assumed about the past unless it can be proven and its practitioners take a very sniffy view of those who jump to conclusions without sufficient evidence. There is a barely polite dispute going on in Israel at present about the significance of finds which are reputed to tell us where King David built his temple. David was an Old Testament biblical figure who, if he existed at all, lived a thousand years before Joseph and Jesus, so evidence is even harder to come by of where he lived and what he achieved. That has not stopped archaeologists from looking for evidence and making claims which are in turn challenged by other academics, who just about manage to avoid referring to their colleagues as charlatans.[4]

Did Joseph really come to Britain with the young Jesus? In Cornwall, they claim, without a shred of solid evidence, that he did so and that he traded for tin with the local miners.[5] Joseph and Jesus can even be seen on the coat of arms of the Cornish fishing town of Looe near where they supposedly arrived. If Jesus was just a boy when Joseph brought him to these shores, Joseph could not have been a missionary because Christianity had not started.

Or did he arrive after the crucifixion, bringing the Holy Grail with him? In this case, Jesus, who was already dead and had presumably ascended to Heaven, could not have come with him and the idea of Christ setting foot in England is impossible. Joseph could, of course, have come more than once, first with Christ and later without him, spreading the message of Christianity after the crucifixion. However, according to Google Maps, it is over two thousand miles from Jerusalem to Glastonbury, an impossibly long journey once in a lifetime in the ancient world, let alone twice. We must consign the supposed journey – or journeys – of Joseph of Arimathea to Glastonbury into the realms of myth.

It is not the purpose of this book to separate what is history and what is legend but to look at the history *of* the legend. William Blake did not concern himself overmuch with the logistics of Joseph of Arimathea's travel arrangements but concentrated instead on the legend. In fact, the two concepts of history and legend were virtually indistinguishable for him, as they were many people in medieval times when faith was more important than fact. Blake's visions of people and angels were just as real to him – and far more important – than those whom he mixed with on an everyday basis. However, even Blake must have known that the idea of Christ coming to England so long ago had to be considered dubious.

This must be why his poem starts with a series of questions rather than statements, introducing an element of doubt and mystery. Blake does not dogmatically state:

> *And those feet in ancient times did*
> *Walk upon England's mountains green.*
> *And the holy lamb of God was*
> *On England's pleasant pastures seen.*

This version does not scan so well but the rhyme remains. However, it is the fact that the poet is asking questions rather than making statements that gives the poem its great power.

Jerusalem may be sung at the Last Night of the Proms when the audience wave their flags around but it is not a "tread the enemy into the dirt because we are better than everybody else" type of song, which many other national anthems are. Even *God Save the Queen*, which sounds like it is a "please look after our dear monarch" song has a pretty vicious second verse in which the deity is asked to "scatter her (or his) enemies/and make them fall".[6] In case God's support of the United Kingdom is in doubt he is invoked to "confound their politics" and "frustrate their knavish tricks". No wonder that Prince Charles has referred to the "politically incorrect second verse" of the anthem, which is hardly ever sung these days.

Britain's official national anthem came into being in 1745 when an alternative monarchy was being offered by the exiled Stuarts north of the border in Scotland to those who were less than impressed with the Hanoverians on the throne at the time. They had been imported from Germany to keep the Catholic Stuarts, who had a far better claim to the crown, away in exile.

When the dashing Prince Charles Edward Stuart, usually referred to as Bonnie Prince Charlie, arrived in Scotland to reclaim the throne for the Stuarts, things were looking decidedly shaky for the sitting monarch George II. Although he was not fighting to gain the crown for himself but for his father, who was still in exile and had not sanctioned his son's escapade, Charles expected to inherit the throne eventually. After his defeat at the Battle of Culloden outside Inverness the following year, the pesky Stuarts ceased to be a serious threat to the established Protestant order and the prince returned to exile.

Bonnie Prince Charlie's early and unexpected successes in Scotland, however, and his growing popularity led many people who felt that the United Kingdom needed a Protestant monarch (whether he spoke with a German accent or not) to proclaim their loyalty to the music of Frederick Arne, who had also written the music for that other jingoistic song *Rule Britannia.* No one knows who wrote the words but the song which was to become Great Britain's national anthem was first sung at the Covent Garden Theatre in London a week after the Prince and his Jacobite army had won a surprise victory at Prestonpans just outside Edinburgh and proceeded to march into the Scottish capital from which they would later descend into England. At this time the House of Hanover seemed to be under real threat and, although there was no specific reference to the rebellious Scots in the music (that came from a verse inserted much later) nobody who sang the words of the second verse could have been in much doubt about who the "enemies" referred to in it were meant to be.[7]

Blake was born in 1757, thirteen years after the Battle of Culloden, at a time when the clearances were emptying the highlands of people in favour of more profitable sheep farming and anything that marked you out as Scottish and potentially rebellious was banned. Not until Queen Victoria came to the throne ten years after his death and fell in love with the Scottish highlands was it considered officially acceptable, even fashionable, to wear the kilt again. No battle has been fought on British soil since Culloden but hostilities between England and Scotland are resumed annually on the sports field. When an English rugby or soccer team ventures north of the border they are greeted with a lusty rendition of the unofficial Scottish national anthem *Flower of Scotland*, a song inspired by the defeat and slaughter of "proud Edward's army" by Robert the Bruce at the Battle of Bannockburn in 1314. The Scots are a warlike lot and in many ways define themselves by their enmity with England.

The English meanwhile sing *Jerusalem*, not as a way of doing down their neighbours, but of rebuilding their own house in a better way. And they do so in the words of a poet and painter who imagined that the young Jesus may have come to England carried on the back of one who may have been his uncle, who is said to have built the first Christian church in these islands and who may even have buried the Holy Grail somewhere near the church and where a thorn tree still flowers twice a year. If Jesus did indeed come to England – highly unlikely at a time when few people travelled such huge distances – then for a short time we had a Jerusalem, our own sacred piece of Heaven in England. This is what Blake wanted to rebuild and what we sing about when we join in the verses of the song we call *Jerusalem*.

Notes

1. Bryant, E. A. and Haslett, S. K. (2002). Was the AD 1607 Coastal Flooding Event in the Severn Estuary and Bristol Channel UK Due to a Tsunami? *Archaeology in the Severn Estuary 13.* Vol 13, pp. 163-167. https://doi.org/10.5284/1069499.

2. research.reading.ac.uk/glastonburyabbeyarchaeology/

digital/arthurs-tomb-c-1331/

3. https://www.glastonburyabbey.com/king-arthur-avalon.
   php

4. The veracity of the King David discoveries and the disputes arising from them is discussed in an aptly named article *Built on Sand* in The New Yorker, 29 June 2020.

5. *Folklore of Cornwall* by Tony Deane and Tony Shaw, chapter two, *The Tinners*.

6. The second verse of *God Save the Queen* in full is:
   "O Lord our God arise,
   Scatter our enemies,
   And make them fall!
   Confound their politics,
   Frustrate their knavish tricks,
   On Thee our hopes we fix,
   God save us all!"

7. There is more discussion of the origins of the official national anthem by Alastair McConnachie at http://www.aforceforgood.org.uk/precious/anthem1

Chapter 3

Fight for Right

Twenty of Britain's fifty-five Prime Ministers have attended Eton College, including two of the last three. Eton is called a "college" but is really a private boarding school for boys. (A few of the 160 teachers are female, but none of the students are.) Everyone who studies there has to prove their academic credentials by taking the Common Entrance examination. If they pass, their families will then have to cough up the fees which come to over £40,000 a year. If you can afford it, there are worse ways to be educated. Every boy studying at Eton gets a laptop and an email address as well as a room of their own to live in while they study at the school. Many go on to Oxford and Cambridge, particularly Christchurch and King's Colleges, both of which have long-standing links with this famous private school.[1]

King's College, Cambridge was founded by that saintly but ineffective King Henry VI, who also founded Eton and endowed scholarships that still pay the fees of seventy boys there. The royal family have several connections with Eton, which is just across the River Thames from Windsor Castle. Prince Charles (who did not need any help with fees) was sent to Gordonstoun in Scotland at the insistence of his father, Prince Philip, who credited it with having supported him through a time of crisis when his mother and several other members of his family had died in a plane crash. Charles, however, was reportedly unhappy with the spartan regime that prevailed in the Scottish Highlands and sent his own sons to Eton.

One of the boys who studied at Eton and often walked over to Windsor was Hubert Parry. He had been sent to the school by his father Gambier Parry, a successful businessman with the

East India Company. Gambier had remarried a few years after the loss of his first wife, who died soon after Hubert was born. With a father often away on business and a stepmother tied up with her own children, Hubert endured a lonely childhood and threw himself into music.

From Eton, he would go to Windsor and study with George Elvey, the long-serving organist of Saint George's Chapel inside the castle. Although he later moved away from Elvey's influence, the organist was an important supporter of the young Parry's musical ambitions, allowing him to write anthems for the choir of Saint George's and helping him prepare for a music degree at Oxford. Parry went on to become the youngest person to pass the Oxford Bachelor of Music exam.[2]

Hubert Parry's musical talent, apparent from a young age, was tolerated by his father Gambier, who had himself appreciated and enjoyed both music and painting without seeing either as a career option for a serious young man in late Victorian England. So Parry did not study music when he went to Exeter College, Oxford reading Law and History instead. Hubert's elder brother had gone off the rails while at Oxford and had been sent down (effectively kicked out) of the university, but Hubert's was of a more obedient and easily tamed nature and he dutifully completed his studies in subjects effectively chosen for him.

A century later another young man threw himself into music after the early death of his mother. His father had been a semi-professional musician and encouraged his son's talents, helping him learn to play several instruments without expecting him to build a career from his musical ability. He was a choirboy and a good student at his grammar school, intelligent and conscientious enough to have realistically aspired to go to university and progress on to a salaried career. In July 1957, however, Paul McCartney met John Lennon, whose band the Quarrymen were playing at a church fete in a Liverpool suburb, and all that soon changed.

Hubert Parry was never led astray by a Lennon and, after he had left Oxford, he did try to follow the career in finance which his father and his wife's family were keen for him to embark on. In 1872, he married Elizabeth Herbert, the daughter of the politician Sidney Herbert, whose statue stands next to that of his friend and protégé Florence Nightingale as part of the Crimean War Memorial in Pall Mall. Herbert had died ten years before but his influence reached out and, in order to join this influential family and to keep his own father happy, Parry joined Lloyds of London as an insurance underwriter in 1870 and remained there for seven years.

He was unsuited to work in the City, however, and music was never far from Parry's mind so it was only a matter of time before its pull proved to be stronger than that of finance. Once released from the grind of office work and allowed to concentrate on music, Parry grew wings. In a busy and productive career, he set works by Shelley and Milton to music, composed five symphonies and a piano concerto, which was performed at the then popular music venue at Crystal Place in South London. He joined the staff of the Royal College of Music when it was opened in 1883, became Professor of Music at Oxford and wrote extensively, including a biography of Johann Sebastian Bach and the third volume of the Oxford History of Music, which covered the seventeenth century. He also composed shorter works, two of the most famous of which are the coronation anthem *I Was Glad* and the tune *Repton*, which is used to accompany the well-known hymn *Dear Lord and Father of Mankind*, with words written by John Greenleaf Whittier. Parry is said to be Prince Charles's favourite composer, although whether Charles will ever hear the anthem *I Was Glad* at his own coronation remains uncertain at the time of writing.

By far his most famous contribution to music, however, was also one of his last. On medical advice Parry had resigned as Professor of Music at Oxford in 1908 and had cut back on his teaching, concentrating more on composition in the last decade of his life. Although he lightened his bureaucratic duties as he grew older, Parry was always something of a workaholic.[3] In 1916, two years before he died and during the darkest days of the First World War, he agreed to set William Blake's poem *Jerusalem* to music. The promise of 1914 that the war would be "over by Christmas" was ringing hollow at the time as both armies were stuck in muddy a stalemate in the trenches.

Fighting had briefly stopped on Christmas Day 1914 with the famous and surprisingly widespread but informal truce between British and German soldiers, who stopped firing at each other, climbed out of the trenches, exchanged cigarettes and gifts, showed each other family photographs and kicked a football or two around for a few hours. Hostilities soon resumed, however, and the officers made sure that no temporary truce was ever allowed to take place again. The German enemy had thenceforth to be portrayed as irredeemably evil and only fit for slaughter, preferably in large numbers.

Parry did not share the anti-German sentiment of so many of his fellow countrymen. He had been brought up on the music of composers such as Beethoven, Bach and Mozart, had attended early performances of Wagner and retained an early love for Mendelssohn. No country has contributed as much to the classical music canon as Germany and a man like Parry, who had dedicated his life to music, would be unlikely to forget this. How could that most cultured country be condemned outright, its people regarded as barbarians?

Nevertheless, Parry put his personal love for Germany and its music aside when asked to do his patriotic duty in 1916. The man who asked him was an old Eton and Oxford friend Robert Bridges, who was the Poet Laureate at the time. Bridges, who is not read as much these days as when he was alive, worked as a doctor before he devoted his life to poetry. He is mainly famous today for championing the work of his fellow poet and

Oxford contemporary Gerald Manley Hopkins, whose poems he arranged to have published nearly three decades after Hopkins' death in obscurity. While Bridges rose to become Poet Laureate, Hopkins was a religious and sexual outsider (he was gay) as well as a Roman Catholic priest. He was unknown in his own lifetime but is much admired today – like William Blake.

Bridges had been at Eton with Parry, who had set some of his poems to music, and the two men remained on good terms. Parry was persuaded by Bridges to become involved in the Fight for Right movement which had been founded in August 1915 to garner support for British troops and to promote the moral superiority of the British cause during the war. It was based at Wellington House, a large government building in central London (now demolished). The movement had been founded by Sir Francis Younghusband, an interesting Edwardian character who had been an explorer, mountaineer and soldier. Younghusband, like many of his contemporaries, was convinced of the need to defeat Germany both militarily and morally and roped in many of the major writers and artistic figures of the day into his Fight for Right campaign.

Thomas Hardy, H G Wells, John Buchan, G K Chesterton and Arthur Conan Doyle all agreed to help with this propaganda push and to support the war effort. Edward Elgar also came on board and wrote the music (but not the words) for the anthem used by the movement. There is no evidence to indicate that any of these writers or composers were subject to overbearing pressure from the government in their public support for the war effort. Men like Elgar, Hardy and Wells had come from humble backgrounds and, at a time when both class distinction and patriotism were the order of the day, they may not have wanted to give critics an excuse to draw attention to their outsider status. Consequently, they put aside any doubts they may have had, fell into line and did their patriotic duty.

While writers who were too old to fight helped the war effort with their pens, younger ones took up the sword, or at least a gun. Wilfred Owen had been a minor poet before the war began but, aided by the support of his fellow officer-poet Siegfried Sassoon, he came of age when exposed to the reality of life and death in the trenches. Owen was to be devoured by the war which had helped him find his voice and was killed in the final days of the fighting, cut down as he led his men across a canal just a week before the armistice was signed. Despite their hatred of the war, soldier-poets like Owen could never be accused of cowardice and willingly led their men into battle. In a bitter irony, his family were able to celebrate the ending of the war shortly before receiving the telegram that informed them of his death.

Another man who might have been expected to give unequivocal support to the war effort was Rudyard Kipling. He had supported the British government at the time of the Boer War and when hostilities with Germany started in 1914. However, he cried off from the Fight for Right campaign, citing ill health. This may have been a cover for his own growing doubts about the war. The memory of his own son John's death, and the part he played in it, ensuring that the younger Kipling was accepted into the army when his eyesight obviously made him unsuitable for fighting, may have haunted him so much that he could not bring himself to encourage other young men to make the same sacrifice. Kipling was later to write: "If any question why we died / Tell them, because our fathers lied".[4] Perhaps a combination of guilt, grief and doubt kept Kipling silent at a time when other writers and artists shelved their doubts and supported the government's propaganda effort.

This unquestioning patriotism all makes a marked contrast with the attitude of writers today when opposing war is a mark of pride and supporting one almost a guarantee of career death. Novelists like Salman Rushdie may have honed their skills in advertising agencies but they are almost always unwilling to use those talents to sell foreign wars to the public. During the First and Second World Wars, most writers could be relied on to support the fight against Germany and more or less toed the official line, even if poets like Owen and Sassoon also communicated the unflinching reality of fighting and dying in the trenches.

A genre that might somewhat gruesomely be termed "corpse poetry", in which a poet reflects on the life lost while looking at the body of a dead soldier, grew up as wartime poets wrote about life in the trenches. Owen drew attention to the contrast between the reality and the romance of warfare in his famous poem *Dulce et Decorum Est* when he describes a gas attack on his troops and the condition of one of its victims as his dead body is thrown into a cart. He even goes so far as to describe the words of Horace, usually translated as "it is sweet and fitting to die for one's country", as "the old lie", which is hardly the sort of message inclined to recommend itself to the Fight for Right movement.

This type of poetry developed further during the Second World War, when the evils of Nazism were enough to lead most non-German writers to either fight or support the war against it, even if W H Auden declined to return to Britain from the USA where he was living. The poetry changed now so that even an enemy combatant came to be seen as a fully-fledged human being. One of the young poet Keith Douglas's most powerful poems is *Vergissmeinnicht* (literally "Forget Me Not") in which he imagines a German soldier and his relationship with his lover, who even has a name, Steffi. He looks at the dead body of this victim of war as it begins the inevitable process of decay and flies gather to do their work, reflecting that "death ... has done the lover mortal hurt". Douglas, like his predecessor Wilfred Owen, was killed in action as the war neared its end. He was twenty-four years old, a year younger than Owen. Those whom the gods love die young.[5]

By the time of the war in Vietnam the gap between a noble intention on the part of the invading country (the USA) was in such stark contrast to the reality of life on the ground of the invaded one (Vietnam) that it became impossible for most writers – and many readers – to reconcile a distant end with the chaotic and bloody means on the ground. The poetry of Douglas and Owen was not widely read until after the wars that claimed both their lives had ended but, even in a pre-internet world, information could move faster and more freely from the battlefield to the home front in the 1960s and there was less inclination to cover up both the reality of what the war was doing to Vietnam and how badly it was going.

Many Vietnamese were stubbornly refusing to regard the Americans as liberators and saw them instead as conquerors, the conduct of their young and usually terrified soldiers reinforcing the idea that, if this was liberation, they wanted nothing of it. When Daniel Ellsberg released the Pentagon Papers to the world in 1969, they confirmed what many already suspected, that the American army was fighting an unwinnable war and that the government had systematically lied about both the extent of the war and success of their campaign. Largely as a result of the war in Vietnam, it is almost unknown for writers, artists, musicians or other creatives, as they are called today, to support their government's wars in places like Iraq and Afghanistan.

If films covered Vietnam, they usually portrayed the American soldier as a victim of his own government's incompetent and overbearing urge to impose a western value system onto countries on the other side of the world. The abiding image of the soldier as the victim of Vietnam is of Bruce Dern walking to his death in the ocean at the end of *Black September*, a film in which he unsuccessfully tries to take revenge on the people of his own country by annihilating a large number of them at an American football game. It may just have been acceptable to have fought in the war in Vietnam but not to have supported it politically.

There are, of course, exceptions. John Wayne did use his influence to make a conventional war film about Vietnam called *The Green Berets* in which the Americans are portrayed as heroic and the North Vietnamese as brutal and sadistic. The film was panned by critics but was a commercial success even though the war itself was becoming increasingly unpopular.

After the war was over Sylvester Stallone was to combine the ideas of the American soldier as both victim and hero in the creation of John Rambo, a drifter picked on in his own country who is sent to refight the war in Vietnam by rescuing a large contingent of supposed American prisoners of war who had been cynically ignored by their own government, while at the same time sending large numbers of Vietnamese to their deaths without having to endure so much as a scratch on his own well-toned muscles. Neither Wayne nor Stallone had any first-hand experience of the war in Vietnam – or any other theatre of combat, for that matter. Theirs was a Hollywood version of warfare, not a warrior's one.

Wars like Vietnam were a million miles from the kind of fight envisaged by William Blake in the poem he had written over a century earlier. His battles were to be fought with bows of burning gold and arrows of desire while machine guns and mustard gas were the weapons of choice in the First World War. Between them, Parry and Bridges turned Blake's call to create a new Jerusalem in England, one that was worthy of Jesus himself, into a rallying cry to encourage people to continue fighting an enemy across the channel in Europe. Blake's war was a moral crusade, while the one his poem unintentionally championed was one in which millions of men died painful deaths in the mud, many before they had set eyes on the enemy.

Bridges had come across *Jerusalem* through the writings of an even less-remembered figure than he was to become. Stewart Headlam was a troublesome priest of the type which the Church of England throws up every so often, an other-worldly radical who preaches to and lives amongst the poor and is not afraid to criticise the rich. He was a self-defined Christian Socialist who became rector of Saint Mathew's Church in Bethnal Green in the east end of London. He was an early champion of unpopular causes and, although he had never met him, he put up money for Oscar Wilde's bail when the Irish playwright was charged with gross indecency in 1895. From his pulpit, Headlam would preach on the importance of creating a just and equal society on this earth. This seemed to anticipate the motto of Christian Aid, the charity which says it believes in "life before death", presumably in reply to those who say that the poor should wait patiently and meekly before receiving their reward after they have passed into the next world.

Headlam might have been a pioneering socialist in favour of the common ownership of land and an early member of the left-wing Fabian Society who disapproved of people hoarding their wealth, but he did enjoy a private income of his own (always handy for those with left-wing views). He used his family money to get by when he was in between jobs, which was quite often as he had a Blakeian knack for airing his radical opinions and losing supporters.

Headlam also used his private money to set up and subsidise *The Church Reformer* magazine. This was a monthly publication that printed the views of the short-lived Christian Socialist movement until it ceased publication in 1895. The *Reformer* never made money, which was probably inevitable given the views of its founder and editor, but it did help to bring Blake's vision of an English Jerusalem back into the public eye from obscurity by displaying the words of Blake's poem across its front page.[6] William Blake and Stewart Headlam were soulmates, uncompromising and other-worldly men who were uncomfortable in mainstream society. The poem that Blake wrote and Headlam revived was taken from them by men far less radical than they were and used for purposes neither would have approved of.

Robert Bridges was to be one of these when he joined Younghusband's Fight for Right campaign. He specified to Parry that the tune for *Jerusalem* should be "suitable, simple music" such as to encourage an audience to join in the singing of Blake's words. Blake himself was never a professional musician but is said to have often sung his own poems as songs, providing the accompaniment as he did so. No record of his own music exists, if it was ever written down, but his poetry often has a musical bent to it, so it was not a tall order for Parry to write something that lent itself to public performance.

This first performance was of *Jerusalem* was at a Fight for Right meeting in Queen's Hall on 28 March 1916.[7] Now replaced with an anonymous office building opposite the Algerian embassy and the BBC Headquarters following its destruction in the blitz, Queen's Hall was considered the main concert hall of the British Empire, which still existed when it was built in the late nineteenth century. It had enough room for 3,000 people, seventeen entrances and two orchestras as well as reputedly excellent acoustics. The Hall was the original home of the Promenade Concerts which were begun in 1895 as a series of popular and inexpensive classical music summer concerts by the hall's manager Robert Newman with the young conductor Henry Wood leading the orchestra. After the Queen's Hall was destroyed by a German bomb in May 1941, the Proms, as they became known, were relocated to the Albert Hall. They moved from a venue named after Queen Victoria to one dedicated to the memory of her late husband Prince Albert.

The Proms featured the music of German composers and, despite a call to ban it during the First World War, their work continued to be played. So strong was anti-German sentiment at the time that families throughout Britain changed their names to avoid being identified as Germanic, the most famous alteration being that of the royal family from the rather cumbersome surname of Prince Albert, Saxe-Coburg and Gotha, to the much simpler Windsor, which has been retained since then. The Battenberg family became Mountbattens and even Gustav Holst who, together with his friend and fellow composer Ralph Vaughan Williams, had once been a pupil of Parry's, dropped the "Von" from his original surname to avoid any taint of Germanicism when he volunteered to serve towards the end of the war. Holst was working on his *Planets* suite at around the same time as Parry was writing his setting of *Jerusalem*, but it took much longer for his work to make an impact with the public.

A patriotic British audience needed little encouragement to join in a song that urged them not to cease from mental fight when confronted by a German enemy threatening the sanctity of their green and pleasant land. The concert in which *Jerusalem* was first performed was conducted by Walford Davies, a former pupil of Parry, who had joined Bridges in trying to persuade the composer to lend his expertise to the project of creating a rousing patriotic hymn to encourage the British people to keep their chins up and retain their famed stiff upper lip in the face of seemingly relentless losses during the war. The initial reason for the fighting was, in the words of the American songwriter Paul Simon "long ago forgotten" when he too adapted an earlier work, in this case, the traditional English folk song *Scarborough Fair*. He had come across the song when he spent a year in England in 1965 as a young folk singer working the clubs, until he paired up once more with his childhood friend Art Garfunkel.

There may have been an element of personal pride as well as patriotism in Parry's agreement to compose an accompaniment to Blake's poem in support of Fight for Right. Parry knew that his best years were behind him and the challenge of writing something which could guarantee him a place in history and boost his already declining public reputation might have helped him overcome any doubts he may have felt. He had achieved success but not – yet – greatness and he may have felt that this was his last chance to do so.

Davies quoted Parry's words as: "Here's a tune for you, old chap. Do what you like with it". This sounds blasé, almost offhand, but then Davies added: "He ceased to speak and put his finger on the note D in the second stanza where the words 'O, clouds unfold' break his rhythm. I do not think any word passed about it, yet he made it perfectly clear that this was the one note and the one moment of the song which he treasured".[8] This sounds like a man who knows he has created a winner and may even have guaranteed himself a measure of immortality, but who is also maintaining a typically English stiff upper lip and does not want to be seen to be making too much of a fuss about his latest – and most lasting – achievement.

It was only later that Parry's doubts about the war and the slaughter which accompanied it grew too strong for him to allow his music to be used for jingoistic purposes. For Parry, a Germanophile and a liberal, the contradiction inherent in turning Blake's mystical poem, full of questions and outlandish, unprovable legends, into a rallying cry that would encourage industrialised mass slaughter was too much and he eventually withdrew from the Fight for Right movement a year later in 1917. He may have looked like a bank manager and a pillar of respectable society but, as his daughter Dorothea was to say of him, he was far less conventional than he appeared: "My father was the most naturally unconventional man I have known. He was a Radical, with a very strong bias against Conservatism".[9]

She added that, such were his religious feelings (or lack of them) that he did not even attend her christening. This was despite – maybe because of – the fact that much of his music was composed to be performed in a church. In his early life

Parry had defied his father to become a professional musician. The move was successful and he eventually joined the British establishment, even becoming a baronet in 1902. The need to make a living from an inherently unpredictable profession, however, was never far from his mind. He had to be accepted by the Anglican-inclined establishment so that he could gain commissions and earn enough to support his family. This necessitated giving some kind of lip service to conventional religious observance. Parry's public piety, however, did not necessarily need to extend into his private life when his doubts – and his admiration for that other noted God-doubter Charles Darwin – could be given a freer rein. This may explain why he stayed away from his own daughter's acceptance into the church for which he wrote so much of his music.

When it came to the war against his beloved Germany, Parry did what was expected of him by supporting his own side until private doubts overcame public duty and he withdrew from the Fight for Right a year after he had joined it. It was then that he decided to use the music he had composed and the song he and Blake had jointly but separately created to a new use.

Patriotism's loss was to be feminism's gain.

Notes

1. etoncollege.com/history
2. Jeremy Dibble monograph on British composers of the early twentieth century: (bl.uk/20th-century-music/articles/british-composers-in-the-early-20th-century).
3. Thanks to Ian Russell for information on Parry (private communication with author).
4. Kipling's poem *Epitaphs of the War*
5. *The Deaths of the Poets* by Paul Farley and Michael Simmons Roberts. This book contains passages on the deaths of both Owen and Douglas and on their graves.
6. David Boyle *Jerusalem* ebook, page 35

7. westendatwar.org.uk/page/parrys_jerusalem?path=0p29p
8. Dibble (pages 483/4)
9. Dorothea Ponsonby, article in *The Musical Times*, Volume 97, Number 1359, page 263, May 1956

Chapter 4

From Suffering to Suffrage

Following the 2019 general election women made up just over a third of MPs in the House of Commons: 220 out of 650 or 34%.[1] This was 101 years after they first gained the right to vote with the passing of the Parliament (Qualification of Women) Act of 1918. Even then, after a long campaign for women to be given the vote, they were only entrusted to place a cross next to their preferred candidate if they had passed their thirtieth birthday and were a householder, married to one or had graduated from university. It was to be another ten years before women achieved full equality in the franchise with men after the passing of the Representation of the People (Equal Franchise) Act in 1928[2] when the voting age for women became the same as for men. At the time this was twenty-one, was later reduced to eighteen in 1969 and, in the case of elections for the Welsh Assembly, is now sixteen.

It was a long battle for women to win the right to vote. There had been three electoral reform acts passed by the British parliament in Westminster during the nineteenth century, but none included women in the extensions of the franchise which they introduced. In fact, the first of these, known as the Great Reform Act of 1832, had specifically excluded women from voting. Only three per cent of the population had the property qualification to vote before this act was passed and a few of these were women, the authorities having never previously considered it necessary to prevent them from voting, so unthinkable was the idea. The 1832 Reform Act, therefore, corrected this by specifying that all voters had to be male.

Extensions of the franchise during the nineteenth century were driven by the Chartist movement whose Great Charter of 1838 received three million signatures and demanded the right to universal – but male-only – suffrage, paid MPs and a secret ballot. Many Chartists were sympathetic to the idea of including votes for women in their demands but felt that this was a step too far for the political establishment of the day, who were notoriously reluctant to submit to the overtures of this popular movement. A famous Chartist demonstration in 1848 was held in Kennington in south London and it was intended that it would conclude with a march to Westminster and the presentation of the movement's demands to parliament. The government, however, had no inclination to take notice of its disenfranchised citizens. It recruited 100,000 special constables to control the crowd and dredged up an ancient law to prevent the Chartists from crossing the Thames to Westminster.

It was not just the male political establishment that resisted demands for women to be allowed to vote. Queen Victoria was extremely hostile to women's suffrage, famously calling it "mad, wicked folly". In theory, she was not actively involved in parliamentary matters and the exercise of the royal veto had long fallen in disuse. The last time it was used was when another female monarch Queen Anne had, on her government's advice, vetoed an obscure piece of legislation called the Scottish Militia Bill in 1707. Victoria, however, was not slow to express her opinions to the leaders of governments which the male half of her subjects had elected and, if she had been an enthusiastic supporter of female suffrage, it might have been more widely accepted before she died in 1901.

Victoria was not the only woman opposed to female suffrage. The Primrose League was formed in 1881 by Lord Randolph Churchill after the Conservatives had been defeated by Gladstone's Liberals.[3] The League aimed to promote Conservative principles, the empire and the church and adopted as its symbol the primrose, the favourite flower of their late leader Benjamin Disraeli who, as Prime Minister, had skilfully engineered the Second Reform Act through parliament in 1867. This was something of a pyrrhic victory as voters in the wider franchise established by the Act were often unsympathetic to Conservatism. Women were encouraged to join the League to promote the Conservative Party but its principles did not include allowing them to vote and many of its female members would have been unsympathetic to such an untraditional and potentially subversive idea.

The suffrage movement grew throughout the century, however. John Stuart Mill was a well-known supporter of gender equality and the author of *The Subjection of Women*. Two years after being elected to parliament in 1865, Mill introduced an amendment to the 1867 Reform Act which would have given women the vote. This was easily defeated and there was little inclination on the part of parliament during the remainder of the nineteenth century to deprive men of the exclusive power to elect governments. The Conservative Party was hostile to the idea of women voting and, although the Liberal Party was more sympathetic, the early twentieth century leader of their party, Herbert Asquith, was an implacable opponent. As war approached in 1914 and, in the words of the Foreign Secretary Lord Grey "the lamps are going out over Europe, we shall not see them lit again in our lifetime", the topic was shelved.

Although, the First World War delayed the cause of female suffrage in Britain it also helped to ensure its eventual triumph. While men were away fighting in the trenches women at home took over many of their jobs and proved quite capable of doing them competently, thus convincing many doubters that they were also capable of casting a vote when their time came. The fact that the suffrage movement had voluntarily suspended their campaign at the outbreak of war in order to support the efforts of the troops also added to their credibility and helped to overcome the hostility and disparagement many campaigners had to endure.

This could be very brutal. A famous cartoon shows a picture of a baby crying its eyes out with the caption underneath: "Mummy's a suffragette". Women who wanted to vote were portrayed as unfeminine, bad mothers and disobedient wives. Other cartoons showed women campaigning for the vote as man-hating harridans and men who supported them as wimps and fools. Opponents of women's suffrage had no hesitation in trying to arouse feelings of guilt and shame amongst those who campaigned for a right that we now take for granted.

Today we think of feminism and pacifism as natural bedfellows but women campaigning for female suffrage often felt that they had to prove themselves to be responsible citizens in order to demonstrate that they were worthy of being given the vote. For many, this meant being good patriots and supporting the war effort. Some women did so by handing out white feathers to men they considered – often on very slender evidence – to be shirking their patriotic duty. These infamous marks of cowardice were presented to any man who was not conspicuously dressed in military uniform when travelling on public transport, or simply minding their own business walking down the street. Even servicemen who been decorated for bravery, such as the seaman George Samson, who had won the Victoria Cross at Gallipoli, were not immune. Samson was actually on his way to a public reception in his honour when he was given a white feather. Some supporters of female suffrage were also pacifists but there was more overlap between support for the war effort and support for women voting than many modern feminists would be happy to admit.[4]

What do we call these supporters of women being given the right to vote? The word "suffragette" has won the battle of history and is now used as the catch-all term to describe those who campaigned for this right. In fact, there were two categories of those who campaigned for women's voting rights: moderate suffragists and militant suffragettes. The contrast is encapsulated in the two organisations which represented their views. These were the suffragist National Union of Women's Suffrage Societies (NUWSS) and the suffragette Women's Social and Political Union (WSPU). The NUWSS boasted a membership of over 100,000 people and encouraged men to support their cause. In February 1907, it organised what became known as the "mud march" when thousands of women marched along Piccadilly to the Strand from Hyde Park on a day of pouring rain. The rain from above and the mud from below, however, did not dampen their feelings or deter them from making their demands known to the male establishment of the day.

Persuasion and petitions, however, were not enough for the WSPU which had been founded in 1903 by Emmeline Pankhurst in her home town of Manchester with the motto "deeds, not words". The WSPU did not admit men into its ranks and its all-female membership did not believe in asking politely for what they felt they were entitled to. Instead, they adopted aggressive campaigning methods, posting letter bombs, going on hunger strikes and then being brutally force-fed in prison. Under the infamous "Cat and Mouse" Act of 1913 suffragette hunger-strikers could be released from prison and, once their health had been restored, they could find themselves re-imprisoned for the offence they had first committed.

The suffragette Emily Davison even lost her life for the suffragette cause. She threw herself in front of the horses running in the Derby in 1913, lost consciousness and never recovered. Thousands of people watched her funeral procession in London but it was to be almost five years before Davison's death was vindicated when women were granted a limited right to vote and another ten years before they achieved full voting equality with men.[5]

Emmeline Pankhurst died just weeks before the act which granted women the same status as men at the polling booth was passed in 1928. This mother of the suffragette movement became increasingly a small c conservative figure who, shortly before her death, was adopted by the capital C Conservative party as a parliamentary candidate. She encouraged her supporters not to look "dowdy" and to dress well, as she always did. Portraits of her show Mrs Pankhurst, who had taken her husband's name on marriage, as a typical elegant and respectable woman of the late Victorian or Edwardian period. She was the opposite of the caricature of a modern feminist, the dungaree-wearing, man-hating woman who has no time for domesticity. Rather, the garment most closely associated with the movement was the "suffragette sash" in the colours of green, purple and white, representing respectively hope, dignity and purity. This last quality is not one you would expect many modern feminist campaigns to endorse but it was considered essential by the suffrage movement.

Emmeline Pankhurst's attitudes to female purity and the duties of women in wartime caused friction in both the suffragette movement and in her own family. She felt sure that the movement had to put its aims on hold at the outbreak of the First World War in order to support the brave young men who were fighting in the trenches. She accused those who did not support her of being disloyal, while they saw Pankhurst as dictatorial and domineering. Her eldest daughter Christabel remained loyal to her mother and the cause but there were rifts between Emmeline and her two younger daughters, Sylvia and Adela. Adela went to Australia after a family row and Sylvia lived with an Italian man without marrying him and had a child out of wedlock at the age of forty-five, much to her mother's horror. Emmeline Pankhurst died a year later and many see Sylvia's break with her mother and rejection of her values as contributing to the older woman's death at the age of sixty-nine.

While her younger daughters embraced left-wing causes, Emmeline Pankhurst retreated from socialism and the Labour party, which she had earlier supported, but which she felt did not do enough for female suffrage. Both Emmeline and Christabel had hopes of becoming MPs, but neither of them achieved their ambition. Christabel had stood as a candidate for the newly formed Women's Party in 1918 but was narrowly defeated by her Labour opponent, while Emmeline was denied the chance to stand for election by her own death ten years later.

Women had gained the right to become MPs after the war ended with the Parliament (Qualification of Women) Act, which was passed ten days after the armistice was signed in November 1918. The first woman to be elected to Westminster as an MP was Countess Markiewicz who was elected to represent a constituency in Dublin (then still part of the United Kingdom) in the general election of December 1918. The countess, whose title came from her Polish husband, had been one of those who had taken part in the Easter Uprising, which was intended to free Ireland from British rule but which ended up leading to the division of Ireland following two brutal civil wars.

Supporters of Irish independence from Britain had not shown the same forbearance as the supporters of women's suffrage when war broke out. In 1914, the British parliament had agreed in principle to grant home rule to Ireland but decreed that the Irish would have to wait until hostilities had ceased before this could be completed. However, the government realised that introducing conscription in parts of Ireland where many people did not feel any loyalty to the crown would be unpopular and unsustainable. Therefore, the British government did not try to force Irishmen into wearing the uniform of the British army, which many of them would have regarded as an occupying force. The upshot of this was that those men who supported British rule in Ireland mostly volunteered to fight, while those who did not were left to their own devices as Britain's attentions were turned towards the war in Europe. In the words of an old Irish saying, "Britain's difficulty is Ireland's opportunity" and so Irish republicans, led by men like Patrick Pearse and John

Connolly, seized control of Dublin and proclaimed the creation of a new country free from British rule from the steps of the General Post Office.

You can still see the bullet marks left on the outside of this building if you go to Dublin today. The uprising did not last long as the British army soon arrived and retook the city within days. The rebels probably knew that they had little chance of success as they did not enjoy widespread support from the Irish people as a whole. Many were executed at Kilmainham Gaol in the city by a British government that had little patience with their rebellion during a time of war. However, the men who were shot soon became martyrs and heroes of the cause of Irish freedom from British rule. In sacrificing their lives they had lit the flame of a fire that Britain was unable to extinguish and they are commemorated every year by all the major political figures in the Irish republic. It is at least arguable, however, that had they not taken over the city of Dublin on Easter Monday in 1916, then Ireland would not have been divided in two and today would still be united – and independent of Britain.

Countess Markiewicz had taken part in the Easter Uprising and was incarcerated in Holloway Women's Prison at the time of her election. She would not have taken her seat in parliament in any case as doing so would have necessitated taking an oath of loyalty to the crown, an act that was (and still is) anathema to an Irish republican. She never sat as an MP in Westminster, therefore, but was later elected to the parliament of the Irish Free State and became the country's first woman cabinet minister. When she died in 1927, she was buried at the national cemetery at Glasnevin in Dublin near other heroes of the independence movement. Eamon de Valera, who later transformed the Free State into the Irish Republic, and who was to be buried in the same cemetery, gave the oration at her funeral.

The first woman to actually take her seat in Westminster as an MP was Nancy Astor, an American born woman who, like Markiewicz, had gained her title by marrying into the aristocracy. She won her husband's old seat of Plymouth Sutton in 1919 when he ascended to the House of Lords as this made him ineligible to sit in the House of Commons. Lady Astor represented this constituency for nearly thirty years until 1945, when she retired. This formidable woman, a lifelong teetotaller, knew how to address and control a crowd and was pictured visiting the devastated centre of Plymouth after a bombing raid during the Second World War. She remains one of Plymouth's most fondly remembered MPs.

Although the movement which had paved the way for women to vote and serve as MPs was often condemned as extremist, it did not take long for Emmeline Pankhurst to join the establishment. In 1930, just two years after she had died, Prime Minister Stanley Baldwin unveiled a statue of her in Victoria Palace Gardens near the Houses of Parliament, a fitting place to commemorate the woman who had campaigned so hard for the right of half the population of the United Kingdom to have the vote. Baldwin and Pankhurst were both members of the Conservative Party and he honoured her by saying that she had "won a niche in the Temple of Fame which will last for all time".

Her memory may last for all time – and she has even been portrayed by Meryl Streep in the film *Suffragette* – but you have to look carefully if you want to pay homage to Emmeline Pankhurst at her statue in Westminster. Go just beyond the large square tower through which the Queen enters when she comes to open Parliament. This is called the Victoria Tower and is at the opposite end of the building to Big Ben. In the park just beyond you can see her statue adorned with symbols of the WSPU. While Pankhurst was honoured with a statue safely tucked away beside the Palace of Westminster, pride of place was later given to the more moderate suffragist campaigner Dame Millicent Fawcett. By this time Britain was being governed by its second female Prime Minister, the first being Margaret Thatcher, who held the job for eleven and a half years, the longest unbroken period since universal suffrage was established. The UK's second woman Prime Minister was Theresa May, who held the office for the rather less impressive time of three years.

It was Mrs May who unveiled Millicent Fawcett's statue in 2018 on the centenary of the passing of the act which first granted votes to women. Like Mrs Thatcher, she was a Conservative and, also like her, Theresa Brasier had adopted her husband's name at the time of her marriage to Philip May. Fawcett's was the first statue of a woman erected in Parliament Square and it was sculpted by a female artist, Gillian Wearing. It stands opposite Big Ben and next to that of Mahatma Gandhi with Nelson Mandela and a few DWMs (dead white males) nearby. Theresa May paid tribute to Fawcett by saying, "I would not be standing here today as Prime Minister, no female MPs would have taken their seats in parliament ... were it not for one truly great woman, Dame Millicent Fawcett."

The campaign to commemorate Millicent Fawcett was led by Caroline Criado Perez who has long pushed for greater recognition of women in public monuments – and has been subjected to death and rape threats as a result. In an article she wrote, Criado-Perez estimated that only 2.7 per cent of British statues are of women who are neither royal, naked nor allegorical.[6] This is something of a minefield for researchers because there are fifty-nine women represented on the plinth of Fawcett's monument, including Emmeline Pankhurst and two of her daughters. Although they are only shown in photographs, if you count these then the arithmetic changes dramatically.

Fawcett came from a family of independent, strong-minded women. Her sister Elizabeth Garrett Anderson was the first woman to qualify as a doctor in Britain and had a female-only hospital named after her. Margaret Thatcher was reportedly keen to keep the Elizabeth Garret Anderson Hospital as an independent entity until the pressures of health service logistics meant that it was absorbed into University College Hospital, where a wing of the larger hospital was named after Britain's first female doctor.[7]

Cynics say that Fawcett's statue shows her folding up a dishcloth as though she had just finished the washing up, like a good housewife. In fact, the banner she holds is inscribed with the words "Courage calls to courage everywhere", a quotation from a speech she made in honour of Emily Davison, who had given her life for the suffragette cause by throwing herself in front of the horses at the Derby. Although Pankhurst had formed the WSPU as a more militant breakaway from the NUWSS, relations between the two women were perfectly cordial and attempts to divide them are unlikely to reveal much except the nature of someone (probably male) trying to divide - and rule - the suffrage movement.

Although she was probably less well known than Emmeline Pankhurst – at least until her statue was unveiled – Millicent Fawcett did make an important contribution to the suffrage cause by persuading her friend Hubert Parry to grant the movement the right to use his setting of *Jerusalem* as their official anthem. Supporters of the cause had already begun singing it informally but permission from the composer was needed for its official use and it was sung with his blessing at a concert on 13 March 1918 in which he acted as conductor. He had originally scored the music for an organ and voices but rescored it for an orchestra.

Parry reassigned his copyright of the music for *Jerusalem* to the NUWSS, Blake's words already being in the public domain by then. (At the time copyright lapsed fifty years after the death of the author, the figure increasing recently to seventy years.) He wrote to Fawcett: "I wish indeed it might become the Women Voters' hymn, as you suggest. People seem to enjoy singing it. And having the vote ought to diffuse a good deal of joy too. So they would combine happily."[8] Here was a chance for Parry to keep alive the song which he, with the help of Walford Davies and Robert Bridges, had popularised. As far as he was concerned, it was no longer the song of Fight for Right and the slaughter of men from the Germany he so admired. Now it was an anthem for a different fight – that of equal voting rights for women.

Parry recalled after the concert that, "the sound of *Jerusalem* when the audience joined in was tremendous".[9] His appearance at this concert was to be one of his last public acts. Parry died eight months after an at least partial victory had been won in the battle for women's suffrage but one month before it was achieved in the war against Germany. He became ill after going on a bicycle ride; a lump developed on his leg, blood poisoning set in and he died at Knightscroft in October 1918.

It is often said that Parry died of the Spanish influenza, although his family say that this was at most a contributory factor in his final illness. The Spanish flu was ripping through Britain at the time, claiming the lives of many of the soldiers who had escaped death in the trenches. This curious name came about simply because Spain was neutral in the First World War. As it was thought that dwelling on the devastation wrought by this outbreak of influenza would be bad for morale, newspapers were told not to carry reports of it in Britain. People were, therefore, largely unaware of the extent of its devastation, particularly amongst soldiers in closely crowded barracks, but they did hear about how it had affected neutral Spain. Hence its name.

As a pillar of the establishment and a noted composer of church music, Parry was buried at Saint Paul's Cathedral. His grave in the crypt is next to that of Arthur Sullivan, another British composer who is known the world over for his popular works, particularly his settings of the words of W S Gilbert in comic operas like *Mikado* and *The Pirates of Penzance*. Sullivan never quite achieved the fame he hoped for and did not become the British Beethoven, as he would have liked. However, he was very productive and, like Parry, wrote music for hymns, the best known being his setting of *Onward Christian Soldiers*.

Parry and Sullivan lie cheek by jowl with artists such as J M W Turner, Henry Moore and Blake's old enemy Joshua Reynolds. Christopher Wren, the architect of the cathedral, also lies nearby underneath his famous epitaph, a suitable one for an architect and one that explains why there is no statue or monument to him anywhere in London: 'si monumentum requiris, circumspice." ("If you wish to see his monument, look around you.") Many military figures such as Lord Nelson and the Duke of Wellington are also buried in the crypt of Saint Paul's. Between Nelson and Wellington, there is also a memorial to (but not the tomb of) Florence Nightingale, who had been supported in her work in the Crimea by Parry's father-in-law Sidney Herbert. You feel that he would have enjoyed her company far more than that of the many military figures surrounding them.

Being a religious non-conformist and relatively unknown at the time of his death, there was no possibility of William Blake being buried at Saint Paul's. There is, however, a memorial to him on the wall of the crypt not far from Parry's grave. It was made by Henry Poole and unveiled in 1927, a hundred years after Blake died. Poole was mainly a creator of war memorials and he must have been busy with them in the 1920s after the carnage of the First World War led to the urge to memorialise those who had lost their lives in it. The Blake memorial was one of his last commissions as he died in 1928, the year after it was unveiled.

Although he was not buried inside the cathedral, Blake's tomb is a fairly short walk away. He lies about a mile to the north in Bunhill Fields near to the graves of other well-known non-conformist writers such as Daniel Defoe and John Bunyan.

On the other side of City Road stands Wesley's Chapel, where another famous dissenter is buried. This was John Wesley, the founder of Methodism, who believed in taking the word of the Bible out to the people by preaching in the open air and who rode thousands of miles on horseback to do so.

"Methodist" was an insulting nickname given to Wesley, his brother Charles and their companions at Oxford University by contemporaries who were sneering at the rigorous and methodical lifestyle they led. However, it was later turned into a mark of pride at their methodical and unfrivolous lifestyle. Shunned by the established Church of England, Wesley continued preaching out of doors to ordinary people, declaring before his death that he considered himself to be still a member of the church that had ostracised him.

Margaret Roberts was brought up in the Methodist Church in her home town of Grantham but became Margaret Thatcher after she was married to Denis Thatcher in Wesley's Chapel. By the time she died in 2013, Mrs Thatcher had become part of the Anglican establishment and her funeral service took place at Saint Paul's Cathedral, the same church where she had been obliged to listen to the Archbishop of Canterbury Robert Runcie remembering the Argentinian as well as the British soldiers who had died in the Falklands War. This was at a service that was supposed to be a celebration of Britain's victory in the war fought in 1982. Mrs Thatcher was later interred next to her husband at Chelsea Hospital, the home for retired soldiers that she and Denis had supported for years. Her preference for being buried in a military setting is a fair indication of her attitude to suspected pacifist priests like Runcie.

Even *Jerusalem* was probably considered a bit too leftish for the saviour of the Falklands so a Methodist hymn by Charles Wesley was sung at Mrs Thatcher's funeral. Parry's music was also played, together with that of other English composers such as Sullivan, Elgar and Holst.[10] Mrs Thatcher's funeral was the first of a British Prime Minister to attract the attendance of the Queen since that of Winston Churchill nearly half a century earlier.

Methodism and Anglicanism have long since buried the hatchet and are now moving towards closer unity. Faced with dwindling congregations, most churches are happy to welcome anyone through their doors these days. The exclusion of those who declined to confirm the thirty-nine articles which defined the Church of England seems alien and pedantic today, although it continued at Oxford University until 1854, long after Blake had died. However, at a time when people were expected to go to church and when atheism was an unusual and potentially subversive attitude, many defined themselves by whether they worshipped at the Church of England or in the chapel. In Somerset Maugham's semi-autobiographical novel *Of Human Bondage*, Philip Carey's aunt, who is married to an Anglican vicar, would cross the street in order to avoid having to acknowledge the wife of the local non-conformist minister.

While Parry was at least a nominal adherent of the established Church of England and thus eligible for burial at Saint Paul's, Blake was a definite dissenter. Much of this was down to class. Parry had been born into privilege and had to fight hard to devote his life to music after he had rejected the safe career in finance that had been set up for him, a move many amongst his contemporaries might have regarded as a downward step towards the dreaded area known as "trade". Blake, in contrast, had always had to work hard to make a living as a tradesman. His parents and he inclined towards the chapel and it was natural that he should be buried near them in the non-conformist graveyard at Bunhill Fields and that his wife Catherine, who outlived him by four years, was then buried nearby.

William and Catherine Blake were buried about seventy metres apart, which might seem like a shame for such a devoted couple, who were rarely more than a few metres from each other when they were alive. However, not only did Catherine say that she did not enjoy much of her husband's company because he was always away in paradise, but the sentimental notion that a couple should be buried next to each other was not something adhered to with much rigour by ordinary people. It was a privilege of the well-off who could afford to commission a fancy tomb in which they would spend eternity lying side by side. During his time in Felpham, Blake may even have gone to the nearby Chichester Cathedral and seen what is now one of the most famous of these, that of the Earl and Countess of Arundel. Philip Larkin wrote a much-loved poem *An Arundel Tomb* about this monument a hundred and fifty years later, commemorating the couple's "faithfulness in effigy" and concluding with the surprisingly upbeat message from a notoriously grumpy poet: "what will survive of us is love".[11] For poorer people like the Blakes, who had little money in this world and less for the next, a joint tomb with a monument like that of the Fitzalan's was out of their league. A simple plot would suffice for their mortal remains.

The story of Blake's grave does not end there because, although a stone was erected in his memory near the monument to Daniel Defoe, the exact location of his grave was uncertain until a Portuguese couple, Luis and Carol Garrido, located it in the early years of the twenty-first century. What was left of William and Catherine was reburied with a new headstone on the one hundred and ninety-first anniversary of his death on 28 August 2018. Many Blake admirers were present, including Bruce Dickinson, frontman for the rock group Iron Maiden. Dickinson deliberately used the present tense when he spoke about Blake at an address to those who had come to honour the poet, saying "William Blake is alive."[12] At the time of writing the Blake Society was even offering offcuts from the planned memorial to him as souvenirs to those prepared to part with forty-five pounds (fifty-five if outside the UK).

Blake's modern admirers have attempted to make up for the fact that he was laid to rest in a humble communal grave without a memorial. This is more to do with their desire to honour him than to comply with his own wishes. His remains were located and funds raised to provide a fitting monument above them. Would Blake, who lived a life of the spirit and who promised his wife that he would always be with her after he had journeyed into the next world have cared to be commemorated in this worldly way? That is more doubtful.

In contrast to Blake, Hubert Parry's grave in the crypt of Saint Paul's Cathedral is rarely visited these days. His status gave him a grander tomb than that of Blake, although his wife Elizabeth Maude, who outlived him by sixteen years, is not buried by his side. Parry also wrote some of the music at the most celebrated event held in the cathedral, the wedding of Prince Charles and Lady Diana Spencer in 1981, which featured his anthem *I Was Glad*. This was originally written for the coronation of King Edward VII and it was also sung at the wedding of Charles and Diana's son Prince William to Katherine Middleton at Westminster Abbey thirty years later.

Parry has played a big part in royal events because his setting of *Jerusalem* was the last piece sung at William and Kate's wedding. Strictly speaking, it is a song rather than a hymn because the words do not specifically praise God. Although some churches do not allow it to be sung for this reason, most are not too fussed about the distinction and are only too happy to welcome people in who can join in the singing of a tune they know well enough.

As well as a fancier grave, Parry also had the funds for a grander home than the Blakes could ever have afforded. He built and later lived in Knightscroft House, a comfortable brick building in Rustington in West Sussex, now divided into flats. The house is a short walk from the sea and Parry, who was born further west along the coast in Bournemouth and was a keen sailor, felt at home next to the English Channel. A stone has been erected outside the house by the Rustington Heritage Association and West Sussex County Council with a blue plaque and the inscription: "In this house between 1881 and 1918 lived the musician Hubert Parry (1848 – 1918) composer of the setting of Blake's Jerusalem". Nearby is another blue plaque for the artist Graham Sutherland who lived ten doors down at Green Bushes. Parry may have met the young Sutherland but could not then recognise him as a future artist who would gain notoriety for painting a now-destroyed portrait of Winston Churchill. Sutherland was just a teenager and Parry was in his last years when they were briefly neighbours.

The cottage in Felpham occupied by William and Catherine Blake, and where he probably wrote the words of *Jerusalem*, is about eight miles from Parry's house in Rustington. Just as Blake's admirers have corrected the neglect afforded him at the time of his death by erecting a memorial at Bunhill, so they are converting the Felpham cottage into a study centre and residential home dedicated to his memory. (Progress on this project is covered in the final chapter.) Parry's admirers, meanwhile, have to be content with a blue plaque outside his final home and another at his birthplace in Bournemouth. His stock may have risen through the music he composed to accompany Blake's poem but it has not gone high enough to justify turning a substantial and valuable set of flats into a museum with gift shop. Blake, on the other hand, has now achieved a national treasure status that might have bemused him and his home is undergoing restoration. A gift shop is not planned in this new centre.

Next to Parry's memorial plaque outside Knightscroft House is a more recent one to his wife Elizabeth Maude, placed there by the Rusti Belles Women's Institute which describes itself as a "progressive WI" (Women's Institute). It commemorates "Elizabeth Maud Parry, 1851 – 1933, President of the

Littlehampton National Union of Women's Suffrage Society",
the organisation of which Millicent Fawcett was national leader.
(The Rusti Belles spell Maud without an "e" whereas her family
usually added one.) Fawcett lived near the Parrys and was a
frequent visitor to their house so she had ample opportunity to
work on him to transfer the rights to *Jerusalem* to the NUWSS,
probably with the help of Parry's wife and daughters, all keen
supporters of female suffrage.

Although he was surrounded by these forthright women
in his Rustington home, there is no evidence to suggest that
Parry was henpecked into giving the rights to *Jerusalem* to the
suffrage movement. Parry's biographer Jeremy Dibble believes
that Hubert and Maude Parry did not enjoy a happy marriage
as their relationship progressed.[13] She had little interest in his
music and, although they had been childhood sweethearts and
had to overcome her mother's objections in order to marry, they
seemed to have grown apart rather than together as the marriage
progressed. Theirs may have been a fairly distant marriage by
the end of his life, but both Parrys were agreed on the rightness
of the cause of suffrage and he was pleased to find a new use for
his setting of Blake's poem.

Whatever the nature of their relationship, Hubert and Maude
Parry continued to dwell under the same roof and to welcome
Millicent Fawcett as a frequent guest in their home. She lived
nearby, her late husband having been MP for Brighton, and she
chose to celebrate the first Act of Parliament granting of votes
to women in 1918 by coming to Littlehampton to meet with the
Parrys. Fawcett had received hundreds of invitations from all
over the country to commemorate this event but she chose to
appear on stage with Sir Hubert and Lady Parry, a recognition
of how much they meant to both the movement and to her.

West Sussex, with its large proportion of retired people,
has a reputation for being a small c conservative area (capital
C Conservative too when it comes to elections). However, it

also produced many supporters of women's suffrage, women like Cicely Hale, Mary Neal and Emmeline Pethwick. In 1913, before *Jerusalem* became their anthem, campaigners went on a Pilgrim's March which passed through Rustington on its way towards Brighton. They were led by Maude Parry and met there by Sir Hubert, providing evidence of Parry's support for female suffrage three years before he had written the music for *Jerusalem*.

This Sussex version of support for women's votes was generally moderate suffragist rather than militant suffragette. It relished the help of ennobled and respectable couples like the Parrys and could not afford to be tainted by suggestions of homosexuality, for which Edwardian England had no tolerance. Henry LaBouchere had introduced a clause into the Criminal Law Amendment Bill of 1885 designed to raise the age of consent to protect young girls from exploitation and to finally end the death penalty for male homosexual acts, which had been on the statute books since the early sixteenth century but had fallen into disuse. LaBouchere's infamous amendment, however, criminalised acts classified as "gross indecency", a definition so wide that it led to frequent persecution of gay men right up until the eventual decriminalisation of male homosexuality in 1967.[14]

Female homosexuality – lesbianism – was not officially recognised under British law. An attempt to ban it was quietly shelved in 1929 lest discussion of this unthinkable practice in parliament should encourage otherwise innocent women to indulge in it. It is a myth that lesbianism was not criminalised in the nineteenth century because Queen Victoria did not think it possible for two women to have sex together and no one could bring themselves to explain to her that it did indeed happen. The myth probably arose after a gay march in New Zealand began by a statue of Queen Victoria. There are plenty of those in Britain and throughout the Commonwealth so it was not surprising that a march would start near one. How that morphed into the myth of Victoria's outlook on lesbianism is anyone's guess.

Some of the early suffragettes may well have been lesbian in inclination but were careful to keep quiet about it. Mary Neal lived together with Emmeline Pethwick for several years but no hint of scandal was ever attached to their relationship. They were both committed suffragettes but also, through their work with the Esperance Club, enthusiastic preservers and promoters of that most traditional male English activity of Morris dancing. Neal worked with the famous chronicler of folk music and tradition Cecil Sharp but fell out with him partly because Sharp was implacably opposed to female suffrage and she was not the sort of woman to be patronised by a man, no matter how distinguished he was.[15]

Neal and Pethwick must have sung *Jerusalem* at the suffragette marches and rallies they attended, although the words Blake had written and which Parry set to music could never be described as specifically feminist. Blake was familiar with the early years of feminist thought and moved in the same circles as Mary Wollstonecraft, the mother of Mary Shelley and the author of *A Vindication of the Rights of Women*. However, his relationship with Catherine, although very close, was one in which the woman selflessly served the man. Peter Ackroyd in his biography of Blake tells how William once forced his wife to kneel and apologise to his brother Robert after a disagreement between them.[16] This certainly does not sound like the action of a committed feminist. Catherine, having promised to obey her husband in her marriage vows, promptly did so. (Anything for a quiet life, she may have thought.) She had been brought up in a society in which the woman was subservient to the man and did not know anything else. Whatever his views on extending the vote to women – an idea he may even have found absurd – Blake did not encourage Catherine to think or act independently. A good relationship with Blake was based on devotion not disagreement.

In any case, Blake himself would never have been eligible to vote in a parliamentary election during his lifetime. Parliament only took the first tentative steps towards universal suffrage by extending the franchise with the Reform Act of 1832, which was not passed until five years after his death. Blake himself was more interested in paradise than politics, the latter an activity considered the preserve of the landed classes in his day.

However, the words of *Jerusalem* are easy to remember and it was not too much of a stretch to shoehorn them into an anthem sung to promote the cause of female suffrage. That is the great beauty of *Jerusalem*: it could be adopted by radicals and conservatives alike, both camps finding something in it to support their preferences. Radicals love Blake's mystical worldview and his outsider status. Conservatives love his patriotism. Both sides enjoy belting out a good song. It was not hard, therefore, for *Jerusalem* to morph from being a song supporting the war effort in 1916 – definitely a conservative cause – to one used to support votes for women – equally definitely a radical one – in the years following.

The story of the song does not finish with the victory of the suffrage movement, however. After women achieved the right to vote and had gained equality on the franchise, it was later taken up by an organisation more noted for its adherence to conservative views than to radical ones, an organisation identified more with jam than with *Jerusalem*.

Notes

1. Parliament.uk
2. Ibid.
3. empire.co.uk
4. Further discussion of the overlap between the suffrage and white feather movements is at: opendemocracy.net/en/5050/white-feathers-girls-womens-militarism-in-uk/

5. Footage of Davison's sacrifice can be viewed on YouTube. (m.youtube.com/watch?v=um9GV6_AILM)

6. newstatesman.com/politics/feminism/2016/03/i-sorted-uk-s-statues-gender-mere-2.7-cent-are-historical-non-royal-women

7. uclh.nhs.uk

8. *C Hubert Parry: His Life and Music* by Jeremy Dibble (page 485)

9. culturematters.org.uk/index.php/arts/music/item/2254-jerusalem-a-hymn-to-women-s-suffrage

10. You can see the order of service for Mrs Thatcher's funeral at Saint Paul's website: stpauls.co.uk/news-press/latest-news/the-order-of-service-for-the-funeral-of-baroness-thatcher. There is also a fine recording of the cathedral choir singing *Jerusalem* at this site.

11. *An Arundel Tomb* by Philip Larkin was written in 1956 and is in *Whitsun Weddings*. The words quoted are from verse three, line two and the final line of the poem in verse seven, line six.

12. blakesociety.org/wp-content/uploads/2017/08/Blakes-Grave.pdf

13. Dibble (page 92)

14. I am grateful to Andrew Lumsden for information about the LaBouchere amendment.

15. *The Suffragettes at Littlehampton: A Concise History* by Angela Tester

16. Akroyd (page 83)

Chapter 5

Chariots and Calendars

The Women's Institute (WI) originated in Canada after Adelaide Hoodless's son John died at the age of fourteen months in 1889.[1] A conventional mother and housewife (or "homemaker" as she would be called today), Hoodless was galvanised by the death of her young son, probably from meningitis, and campaigned for women to be better educated in hygiene and domestic science. She started to give public lectures on the importance of improving the education of women isolated in their homes. Two former schoolteachers, Erland and Janet Lee, heard Hoodless give one of these talks and Erland suggested setting up an organisation dedicated to women educating and supporting each other. The newly formed Women's Institute had its first meeting at Stoney Creek, Ontario in 1897.

The WI crossed the Atlantic when the recently widowed Madge Watt moved back to Britain from Canada with her sons. She had been an active member in both Ontario and British Columbia and worked with John Nugent Harris of the Agricultural Associations Organisation to kickstart the setting up of WI's in Britain. The first meeting in the UK was held in 1915 on the Isle of Anglesey just off the coast of North Wales, held in a village which the locals call simply Llanfair P G but which has a further claim to fame. In the middle of the nineteenth century, some bright spark had the idea of renaming this small town of 3,000 souls Llanfairpwllgwyngyllgogerychwyrndrobwllllantysiliogogogoch, which was then considered the longest town name in the world. About 200,000 people a year stop there to take a photograph, buy a souvenir and view the railway station sign at the world's ultimate tourist trap.[2]

The fact that the setting up of the Women's Institute in both

Britain and Canada needed the support and backing of two men might raise a few eyebrows today. However, women in the late nineteenth and early twentieth century did not possess anything like the assumption of equality they now enjoy and they needed male support in order to establish themselves and be taken seriously. Women at the time were expected to take their husband's name, bear and raise his children and set a decent meal in front of him when he finished his day's work. Most importantly, they were not allowed to vote and the setting up of the Women's Institute and its branches was tied up with the work of the suffrage movement to win this right. Any woman is now entitled to join the WI but men are not allowed to become members.[3]

One of those who was involved in both the suffrage movement and the starting of the Women's Institutes was Grace Hadow, an early female student at Oxford University who, despite gaining first-class honours in English at the finals examinations of 1903, was not allowed to receive a degree because she was a woman. This did not deter her and she went on to publish several books and to have a successful teaching career at the same university that had once denied her the degree she should have been awarded.

Hadow was a committed suffragist who wrote:

I am glad that I belong to a generation which has been stoned – not because I like being stoned (it is tiresome, and often messy), but since some women had to go through that to win the thing … I record it here because it looks as if one of the results of the war was going to be the grant of the parliamentary franchise to women. In years to come it may interest people to realise that before the war law-abiding and peaceful women like myself, quite inconspicuous members of a political party, got to take being mobbed and insulted as part of the ordinary day's work.

Hadow sent congratulation to Millicent Fawcett when the "the thing" (votes for women) was granted in 1918 and she kept Fawcett's reply for the rest of her life.[4]

Hadow was involved in setting up a WI in her home town of Cirencester, where she also set up a branch of the suffragist NUWSS. She had returned to Cirencester to nurse her elderly mother and, after she died, Hadow became Director of the Welfare Department of the Ministry of Munitions, helping to improve conditions for the thousands of women who were producing ammunition for the soldiers in the trenches. This formidable woman was able to move seamlessly from academia to Whitehall via the suffrage movement and the WI.

It is worth quoting Hadow in full on the role of Women's Institutes and the relationship between them and the fight for members to gain the right to vote:

The essence of Women's Institutes is their apostolic democracy ... The Women's Institute is for all alike; rich and poor, gentle and simple, learned and unlearned - all pay the same subscription, have the same privileges and the same responsibilities. Each member in turn acts as hostess to her fellow members; each puts her own practical knowledge at the service of the rest. Controversial subjects; religious or political are taboo, but interest in their own homes tends naturally and inevitably to interest in questions of housing, sanitation, infant welfare and kindred topics. The members learn to realise their responsibility towards the community in which they live, and, from an interest in their own village and their own country come to see the connection between their affairs and those of the nation at large. It would be difficult to plan a better training for the exercise of the vote - a training entirely divorced from all party or sectarian policies, based on the actual experiences of home life and home needs, and working outwards through a sense of responsibility educated not to take but to give.[5]

Today one might expect a woman with views like this to lean towards left-wing causes, but Hadow, as well as helping to start the WI in Cirencester and campaigning for women's suffrage, was also secretary of the local branch of the Conservative and Unionist Women's Franchise Union. Like Lady Astor and Emmeline Pankhurst, she saw no contradiction between backing the then radical idea that women should have the right to the vote and also being a member and supporter of the Conservative party.

Justified or not, the WI has the reputation for being a small c conservative organisation. Some members slow hand-clapped Tony Blair when, as Labour Prime Minister, he gave a speech at their AGM in 2007. Admittedly, Blair had made the mistake of introducing what sounded like party politics into his speech, but it is difficult to imagine that these same women would have done the same to Margaret Thatcher, whatever she had chosen to say. One withering look from those steely blue eyes would have silenced them. Mrs Thatcher may have had a reputation for being a strong woman but she seemed to have little time for the feminist movement and was famously photographed surrounded by an all-male (and all-white) cabinet when she assumed office in 1979.

Tricia Stewart mentions the Blair incident in her book *Calendar Girl*, about the events which must surely be the most famous in connection with the WI in recent times and which brought this rather sleepy organisation back into the public eye. It is safe to say that, if it had not been for Stewart thinking up the idea for a calendar of mature naked women with parts of their anatomy discreetly covered by items the WI is associated with, then you would almost certainly never have heard of her. She joined her local WI in the Yorkshire village of Cracoe soon after she moved there with her husband and family. Her neighbour Angela Baker knocked on the door and suggested she join, adding that "people in the village would think it funny if I didn't".[6] As a newcomer, anxious to fit in and to be friendly, she realised that joining the local WI was the done thing for women in a rural community in Yorkshire.

Tricia and Angela attended WI meetings in the local hall, or "hut" as it was known, and she enjoyed being part of an organisation she describes as being "the backbone of the country". They were the youngest members of their branch and became close friends. Stewart writes in her book about how older members would scrape their chairs noisily and put the kettle on and rattle the cups if a speaker at one of their meetings went on for too long. Ange and Tricia, as they called each other, would presumably leave the hint-dropping to more senior members.

In the 2003 film *Calendar Girls*, however, it is Tricia and Ange, portrayed by Julie Walters and Helen Mirren as "Chris" and "Annie", who collapse into giggles at the back of the hut when a speaker goes on for too long about his chosen topic. The film, as they say in the movie business, is "based on a true story" but that did not prevent the writer Tim Firth and director Nigel Cole from sexing it up, literally in the case of hints about the secret lives of some of the women. These were invented by the filmmakers to give the story a little extra frisson. Chris and her husband run a floral business rather than a medical supply company and the tensions between members of the group who made the calendar are not touched on at all. However, if not entirely accurate, the story told in *Calendar Girls* is true to the spirit of the women who disrobed and posed so memorably when the calendar was first produced in April 1999. They made and sold the calendar without earning any money for themselves, purely to raise funds to combat the cancer which a year earlier had claimed the life of Angela Baker's husband John, who had worked in the Yorkshire National Park.

Tricia Stewart's original idea for the calendar was simply to raise enough to provide the hospital where John had been treated with a new sofa in his memory. She soon found that the concept took over her life and she is now in demand as a motivational speaker and minor celebrity in her own right, while the widowed Angela prefers to stay more in the background. The story of their friendship and the calendar they produced has migrated from film to stage in a play and later a musical with songs written by Gary Barlow of Take That. So far, the calendar has raised five million pounds for cancer research and been widely imitated by both male and female subjects being photographed in states of semi-nudity. Tricia dedicated her book to her long-suffering husband Ian, who did at least have the consolation of playing guitar with Brian May of Queen, one of many high profile supporters of the calendar project.

Tricia Stewart ruefully says in her book that she had never understood why the Spice Girls and the Beatles, with such seemingly successful formulae, decided to break up and go their separate ways. She knows now. It is not the purpose of this book to analyse all the meowing that went on between the women who posed for the first calendar but it seems that two factions grew up out of the original eleven who posed, each woman representing one month with the whole group together for the final December photograph. The two groups – "the five" and "the six" – split into those who were keen to keep the project going and those who became fed up with the way that the success of the calendar seemed to take up so much of their lives and time. Relations between the two factions became distinctly frosty with newspaper articles rehearsing their differences in public.[7] Further calendars were produced after the original one but, while all of the women still meet at the local WI, the friendships on which the original one was built have been strained or shattered in the process.

Stewart seemed to enjoy the spotlight and – while it should never be said that she ever made any money directly from the calendar itself – she did write a book and build up a separate identity as a motivational speaker in the wake of the calendar's success. This gave her the opportunity to travel to many countries she would never have gone to otherwise and to rub shoulders with Hollywood royalty like Helen Mirren and Julie Walters as well as the real version in Prince Charles and his wife Camilla, both supporters of the calendar project.

Hollywood had already used a phrase from *Jerusalem* in one of its most popular films which, like *Calendar Girls*, was also based on real events, later became a stage play and – most importantly from the film industry's point of view – garnered a tidy profit. Both films brought in around ten times what they cost to make and continue to earn revenue on the small screen. *Chariots of Fire*, however, is pretty much an all-male affair, a few female characters appearing occasionally as supports for their menfolk. (The film definitely does not pass the Bechdel test, for which it would have to feature two women talking to each other about something other than men.) It is based on the story of the British team that went to the Paris Olympics in 1924, the two main strands of the story being those of Harold Abrahams, who had to battle both anti-Semitism and anti-professionalism to win a medal, and Eric Liddell, a devout Scot who seemed to have given up his chance of winning gold by refusing to run in the hundred metre heats which were held on a Sunday. For a devout Presbyterian like Liddell, competing on the Sabbath would have meant betraying his principles. Unable to run at his best event, Liddell eventually won a bronze medal at two hundred metres and gold at four hundred metres in his first serious race at that distance. Women athletes, incidentally, did not compete in athletics at these games, their involvement in the Olympics not really starting in earnest until after the Second World War when the patronisingly named "flying housewife" Fanny Blankers-Koen of Holland won four gold medals at the London games in 1948.

The phrase "chariots of fire" does not actually appear in Blake's poem, although the song is sung by a boys' choir in the film. The poem refers to a "chariot of fire" in the third verse and this phrase comes from the Bible, specifically 2 Kings, chapter two, verse eleven in which a chariot and horses of fire suddenly appear to take the prophet Elijah "by a whirlwind" into Heaven. They later reappear in chapter six, verse seventeen, in which a whole convoy of chariots and horses are seen by another prophet Elisha, a follower of and successor to Elijah.

Blake, who knew the Bible well, was well aware of the origins of the phrase he was using in the poem, one which was later taken up for the title of the film. The late Colin Welland, who wrote the script, had said that the title *Chariots of Fire* was inspired by Blake's poem. He also said to the audience at the 1982 Academy Awards, when he won an Oscar for his script, "the British are coming", an optimistic but not particularly accurate prophesy as it turned out.

Successful British made films are fairly few and far between in Hollywood. However, *Calendar Girls* made nearly twenty years after *Chariots of Fire*, provided a small measure of confirmation for Welland's prediction. Although it had a largely British cast and crew, the film needed Hollywood money in order to be made and some of it is set in the USA, where the Calendar Girls themselves are invited to appear on television. Jay Leno provides a cameo appearance as the talk show host who invited the women onto his show, thus helping to boost the audience figures in the lucrative American market.

In the film, Julie Walters' character is based on Angela Baker, whose husband's death provided the inspiration for the calendar. In real life she was Miss February and is shown playing the piano with the caption "and the countenance divine shone forth", an obvious reference to *Jerusalem*. She was learning to play the piano at the time and the photographer Terry Logan, who was married to one of the models, thought that this would be the right pose for her, although he had to crop the picture to hide her unflatteringly saggy bottom as she had lost a good deal of weight following the death of her husband. The cropped part of this photograph hangs on the wall of her house according to Tricia Stewart, who should know.

Jerusalem is featured in the film with an enthusiastic pianist bashing out the tune as the group gathers for meetings. It has become so closely associated with the WI that, when people refer to "jam and *Jerusalem*", you immediately know they are talking about the Women's Institute. The WI's exclusive rights to the tune lapsed in 1968 when *Jerusalem* entered the public domain in 1968 but it is still often sung at WI meetings.

Members of the WI were first heard singing *Jerusalem* at their AGM as far back as 1924 when the organisation was less than ten years old but well over a hundred branches had already been started throughout Britain. By this time women had gained the vote and were well on the way to achieving equality in the franchise, which was finally granted in 1928.

The combination of being a non-party political organisation and one responding to the desire of women to have a greater identity outside the home struck a chord with British women of the early twentieth century, whatever their political views. Attending WI committee meetings, learning to speak up to make yourself heard and taking notes of decisions made was good training for women who had hitherto been expected to confine themselves to purely domestic duties but were now keen to step into political life as well.

One of those who cut her teeth at the WI and moved on to Westminster was Margaret Winteringham, who was the third woman to be elected as an MP in the UK and the second to take her seat in Westminster after Nancy Astor, with whom she worked to retain women police officers in Britain. Countess Markiewicz had turned down the opportunity to take her seat because of her support for Irish republicanism – not to mention her occupancy of a cell at Holloway Prison at the time of her election. Winteringham was elected to her late husband's seat in Lincolnshire and became the first woman to represent a rural constituency. Whilst showing fellow members of the WI around the Houses of Parliament, she told them that being a member of the Institute was "the best training she could have for being an MP".[8]

Hubert Parry had died in 1918 soon after the rights to his setting of *Jerusalem* were given to the suffrage movement once he had withdrawn them from the Fight for Right campaign. Aware of his sympathies for the cause of female suffrage, the executors of his will granted the WI the rights in 1928. Proprieties had to be observed by the bureaucracy of the new organisation, however, and, following the spontaneous performance of *Jerusalem* at the WI annual general meeting in 1924, the Institute's magazine *Home and Country* ran a competition to choose an official Institute song. Appealing to both left and right-wingers alike and being easy to sing out loud with gusto, *Jerusalem* was the natural choice and was quickly adopted by the WI.

Once the campaign for female voting had achieved its aims by 1928 and the suffrage societies inevitably closed for business soon afterwards, the Women's Institute took possession of the rights to a by now familiar song. On YouTube you can watch an all-female choir of over five thousand women lustily belting it out in the presence of the Queen, her daughter Princess Anne and daughter-in-law Sophie, Countess of Wessex at the 2015 WI centenary meeting in the Albert Hall.[9] Her Maj looks a bit grumpy during the singing, almost as if she would have preferred to hear *God Save the Queen* instead. However, she kept her thoughts to herself, as she always does.

WI members have also been known to sing *Jerusalem* without musical accompaniment outside on the steps of the Albert Memorial if they hold their AGM inside the Hall. Queen Victoria might not have liked the idea of giving women the vote but the monument and hall dedicated to her late husband Albert provide a familiar backdrop to the singing of a song forever associated with an organisation that grew out of the campaign for women's suffrage.

Notes

1. Fiona Hughes of the WI provided help with information about WI and suffrage: thewi.org.uk/__data/assets/pdf_file/0003/145290/The-WI-and-the-Womens-Suffrage-movement.pdf

2. The name translates into English as "The church of Mary of the pool of the white hazels near the rapid whirlpool and the church of Tysilio of the red cave".

3. As far as transgender rights are concerned, the WI seems to have opened its doors to those who have transitioned. Their website says that "anyone living as a woman is welcome to join the WI".

4. Information from Anne Stamper, Honorary Archivist of the National Federation of Women's Institutes.

5. Women's Institutes by Grace Hadow: reprint from the Journal of the Board of Agriculture - Vol XXV no 7 October 1918. (From Stamper, above)

6. *Calendar Girl* by Tricia Stewart (page one)

7. Daily Mail article, 18 May 2009 interview with some of the disaffected group of five

8. Stamper

9. youtube.com/watch?v=k-J1XaLaa_0&list=RDkJ1XaLaa_0&start_radio=1 or just go to youtube.com and type "WI Jerusalem Albert Hall" into their search box and you will be taken to the clip. It lasts for two minutes and thirty-nine seconds.

Chapter 6

Elgar Arrives

Although less than three per cent of the money we spend in Britain is in the form of cash it is still a major honour to be portrayed on one of our banknotes. Edward Elgar had that privilege between 1999 and 2010 on the series E twenty pound note on which his face – and its impressive Edwardian moustache – appeared, with Worcester Cathedral in the background. One hundred and fifty million of these notes were printed, making Elgar worth about three billion pounds, if you assess his value purely in monetary terms.[1]

Money was one thing the young Edward Elgar always seemed short of. Unlike Hubert Parry, he never enjoyed a family income or public school education but had to struggle to earn a living from his earliest days. Writing to a friend in 1884 he said "I have *no money* – not a cent".[2] Elgar had come from a musical background but found it hard to establish himself as a composer. He was born in 1857, thirty years after William Blake died. His father William was a piano tuner who ran a music shop in Worcester but lacked the confidence to perform in public. In contrast, Elgar's mother Ann seems like an assertive woman. She brought the family into the Roman Catholic church so Edward grew up as an outsider, condemned in the eyes of the educated musical establishment as both a Catholic and a tradesman who rode a bicycle and needed to mind the pennies to pay his bills. We might think of Elgar today as a pillar of English conservatism and upholder of tradition, but he had to work hard to establish himself and was almost entirely self-taught in music, an accomplished player of several instruments who had ambitions to go beyond playing into composition but who found the road a hard one to tread.

Elgar took on many workaday musical commissions to pay the bills and one of these was the scoring of *Jerusalem*. The music had been written by Parry six years earlier but it is Elgar's orchestration that is normally used and which you can hear on the recording at the Albert Hall of members of the Women's Institute singing the song that will be forever associated with their organisation in the presence of the Queen, even though they no longer have any exclusive rights to it.

Elgar has much in common with his contemporary Thomas Hardy. Both men came from humble backgrounds, Hardy the son of a stonemason, Elgar of a man who could make a living from music but who would never perform in public. Both started work in an office rather than going to university, Elgar with a solicitor, Hardy in an architect's practice, before moving on to creative work through their determination and talent rather than through any inherited advantages. The resulting works of both men are filled with a late Victorian and Edwardian melancholy as the days of empire begin to draw to a close and the First World War approaches. Elgar and Hardy did their patriotic duty and supported the war effort but Hardy had little enthusiasm for the role of propagandist. He later wrote bitterly: "After two thousand years of mass/We've got as far as poison-gas".[3]

Both Elgar and Hardy married women from a higher rank in society who might have helped to improve their social status. Their marriages worked out differently, however. Edward and Alice Edgar were a devoted couple and she remained by Elgar's side as a constant companion and supporter for better or worse. Like Blake, he had suffered rejection by a previous girlfriend and could find in Alice a source of strength and loyalty such as a younger woman might not have been willing to offer. She, at thirty-seven, probably saw him as a last chance of marriage and was prepared to break with her family who were horrified that she had taken up with her piano teacher who was eight years younger than she was.

Alice's family disinherited her when she went ahead and married Edward but she loyally stood by him and would go out in all weathers to post his manuscripts. She fought his corner as he attempted to establish himself as a composer and chivvied him along when depression set in, as it often did. Alice was happy to be the supporter and servant of a great man and many attribute much of his success to her stubborn belief in him. Elgar was eventually rewarded with many honours and Mrs (later Lady) Elgar enjoyed these as much, probably more, than he did. When she died in 1920, Elgar was bereft and never remarried, spending his last fourteen years as a widower.

Grief of a different sort afflicted Thomas Hardy after the death of his first wife Emma. While Alice Edgar put the class differences between her and Edward behind them, Hardy's wife Emma only emphasised them as she grew older but not closer to Thomas. The Hardys came to live increasingly separate lives at Max Gate, their home in Dorchester and, while his religious doubts grew, Emma embraced the conventions of the church with ever greater determination. After her death in 1912, he married his much younger secretary Florence Dugdale but, instead of enjoying this second marriage to a younger protégé (as T S Eliot was later to do) Hardy looked back regretfully to the love he had shared with Emma and had then lost. Florence's frustration with her husband's mourning was to be literature's gain as Hardy left novel writing behind and wrote wonderful poems of grief and loss in his later years.

While Hardy is one of the many great writers Britain has produced over the centuries, we have never been noted for producing major composers. Elgar is probably our most famous one and he is best known around the world for writing *Pomp and Circumstance*. The tune is familiar to Americans and is played at their high school and college graduation ceremonies, although some may be unaware that it was actually written by an Englishman. The tradition dates back to 1905 when Elgar was given an honorary Doctorate of Music by Yale University and their Professor of Piano, Samuel Sanford, made sure that the tune was played at the event to honour him. Elgar and his wife were in attendance and this seems to have been the first – but certainly not the last – time that the tune was used at a graduation ceremony.[4]

Sanford, incidentally, should not be confused with Stanford. The first was an American admirer of Elgar who gave him a beautiful Steinway piano to play in his house, while Charles Villiers Stanford had been a colleague of Hubert Parry at the Royal College of Music. He taught many aspiring composers but later fell out with both Parry and Elgar and is now a lesser figure than either in the history of British music of the late nineteenth and early twentieth century. This was probably the most productive time for classical music in Britain with Parry and Stanford leading the way, Elgar, Ralph Vaughan Williams and Gustav Holst following behind, the later composers now better known than their predecessors. Vaughan Williams' most famous composition is probably *Lark Ascending*, regularly voted Britain's favourite by listeners to Classic FM, while many otherwise unschooled in orchestral music would recognise parts of Holst's *Planets Suite*.

Elgar stands above them all, however. *Enigma Variations* was his first major public success. It was composed almost by accident as Elgar sat doodling at the piano one day in 1898 and his wife told him it was "a good tune" that she was hearing.[5] Elgar managed to find the music again and out of it grew a series of sketches dedicated to his wife and various friends. These were polished and performed in public within a year and Elgar's reputation was made. He had been born twenty years into the reign of Queen Victoria and, shortly before the Queen died, when Elgar was already in his early forties, he finally established himself in the public's mind as a composer. All that hard work and struggle had paid off and this son of trade and religious outsider could finally look forward to being accepted by the British music-appreciating public and could also enjoy a degree of financial security.

Queen Victoria was succeeded by her eldest son, who took the title of Edward VII. According to legend, it was the new king's suggestion that Elgar's first *Pomp and Circumstance* march be transformed into *Land of Hope and Glory*, enthusiastically belted out by the audience at the Last Night of the Proms just before they sing *Jerusalem*. In fact, it is more likely that the singer Clara Butt, who first sang it in public, had the idea to add words to Elgar's tune and turn it into a song.[6] Whoever had the idea, words were written by the poet A C Benson and the result was ready for Edward's coronation, which had to be delayed because of his ill health. Indeed, many British people must have wondered if Victoria's son would even live to be crowned as her successor.

In the event, Edward arose from his sick bed to be crowned in August 1902. At the ceremony he was given the title King of France as well as Great Britain but, a confirmed Francophile who spoke the language and who had encouraged the entente cordiale between the two countries, he mumbled the words accepting the French crown, which dated back to the days of Henry the Fifth and the Hundred Years War, and they were sensibly dropped for future coronations.[7] Even though there had been a vacancy on the French throne for over a century, the days when an English monarch could cross the Channel with his army to fill it had long passed.

Elgar wrote six *Pomp and Circumstance* marches in all but it is the first that is best known. Its debut performance was in Liverpool in 1901 but it was played soon afterwards in London at a Promenade Concert in the Queen's Hall (the same venue where *Jerusalem* was first sung fifteen years later). It was an immediate success and fulfilled Elgar's prediction that the tune would "knock 'em flat".[8] The orchestra's conductor Henry Wood later recalled that it "was the one and only time in the history of the Promenade concerts that an orchestral item was accorded a double encore".[9] A year later Benson's words were added, the tune was modified and it was used at Edward the Seventh's coronation in Westminster Abbey.

Land of Hope and Glory survives as a popular tune but, with its militaristic words and celebration of empire – one that should spread "wider still and wider" across the globe – it has not achieved quite the widespread affection afforded to *Jerusalem* in the minds of all British people. In the summer of 2020, the BBC announced that *Land of Hope and Glory* will be played but not sung at the Proms. There would be no audience of Promenaders to sing it due to the coronavirus outbreak and what seemed like a sensible practical decision has been interpreted as an old friend (enemy to some) called "political correctness gone mad". Under pressure, the BBC reinstated the singing of an old but not universally popular favourite.

It is impossible to imagine this happening in the case of *Jerusalem*, which appeals to both left and right-wingers alike and has no imperialist connections. For the 2020 Proms, it was rescored in a new arrangement by Errollyn Wallen and dedicated to the so-called Windrush generation of immigrants to Britain from the West Indies, the first of whom arrived in Britain after travelling here in the ship of that name. Wallen is a child of these immigrants, and one who has not let racism hold her back. She was the first black woman whose work was performed at the Proms and she was the first woman to receive the Ivor Novello Award for Classical Music in 2013.[10] She was also awarded an MBE by the British government in 2007. Some people have turned this honour down because the "E" in it stands for "Empire" but she did not consider that sufficient reason to refuse or return her gong.

You can see a memorial to those who arrived on the *Windrush* in the reception centre at Tilbury Docks where the ship berthed in 1948. The square in the centre of Brixton in south London, where many of them ended up living, has been renamed Windrush Square in their honour and a war memorial to the black servicemen and women who fought for Britain in the First and Second World Wars was unveiled in this square in 2017 opposite Lambeth Town Hall. However they have been memorialised today, many immigrants found that the reality of racism in Britain stood in the way of the high hopes they held for a better life here and the words "Windrush" and "racism" often go hand in hand.

Wallen, a black woman, joins Hubert Parry and Edward Elgar, both very much white men, as one of those who have set *Jerusalem* to music for the Promenade Concerts. Elgar's setting of Parry's tune was first performed at the Leeds Music Festival in 1922, and is used more often than Parry's version these days. Unsurprisingly, Parry's biographer Jeremy Dibble thinks this is a pity. He says that Parry's version "has a distinctive quality which gives complete prominence to the tune without the distraction of Elgar's dynamic embellishments".[11]

Elgar himself was well aware of Parry's talents. Ralph Vaughan Williams recalled in a letter,

> *I was once sitting next to Elgar at a rehearsal of Parry's Symphonic Variations. I commented on the curious spiky sound of the orchestra which fascinates me though it may repel others. I said to Elgar, 'I suppose this would be called bad scoring though personally I do not think so.' He turned on me almost fiercely and said, 'Of course it's not bad scoring; that music could not have been scored anyhow else.'*[12]

Elgar's scoring emphasises jingoism in *Jerusalem*, while Parry produced a more restrained, sober version.

Whatever the merits of each composer's setting of *Jerusalem*, it is Elgar who is far better known as a composer today. He was influenced by Parry but the pupil strode beyond the master and, despite not enjoying Parry's privileged upbringing, it is Elgar who ended up on our banknotes. Portraits of both men show them with impressive moustaches and dressed in a suit and tie, as was expected of Edwardian gentlemen. Parry enjoyed sailing, while Elgar preferred land-locked sports like golf, horse-racing and football. Elgar supported Wolverhampton Wanderers and even wrote a song for them, which was revived and performed in aid of a fund-raising event for a Wolverhampton church in 2010.[13]

Both composers also played their part in supporting the war effort from 1914 to 1918. Elgar wrote the music (but not the words) of the patriotic song *Fight for Right*, which was adopted by the campaign of that name while Parry, although he later withdrew his support, first set *Jerusalem* to music for the same organisation. Parry died shortly before this war ended, while Elgar lived on until 1934, by which time Hitler had come to power in Germany and Europe was heading inexorably towards another war. In his later years Elgar became a pioneer of the recording studio and would conduct the orchestra at Abbey Road Studios in London where, later on in its history, groups like Pink Floyd and the Beatles recorded their albums and singles. Abbey Road is famous for the photograph taken in 1969 of John, Paul, George and Ringo walking over the pedestrian crossing outside the studio but it is Elgar's name that is to be seen on the memorial plaque attached to the building.

It is curious, however, that *Jerusalem* is barely mentioned in biographies of Elgar. He is known for *Pomp and Circumstance*, *The Enigma Variations* and his Cello Concerto, which summons up memories for many filmgoers of Emily Watson sawing away in *Hilary and Jackie*, the film about Jacqueline du Pre, who died from multiple sclerosis in 1987. (Watson is very convincing in the role but she did not actually play the music, which was dubbed onto the soundtrack.) Elgar's *First Symphony* was performed over a hundred times in its first year, unlike the Cello Concerto which was badly rehearsed and received and then quietly shelved after a disastrous premiere. Works like *The Dream of Gerontius* and the beautiful *Chanson d'Amour* will also ensure Elgar's immortality, but few people seem to take much notice of the fact that he also gave England's most famous song its usual setting.

This may well be because Elgar's scoring of *Jerusalem* was essentially a reworking of what Parry had first produced six years earlier when it was first sung at the Queen's Hall in 1916. His arrangement of the tune was a new orchestration of what had already been created by the older composer rather than an original work by Elgar himself. Play the two settings one after the other and the untrained ear might not easily be able to distinguish them. Elgar was a working musician, a versatile player of several instruments, including the piano, violin and bassoon, and he produced many scores for orchestras which he often conducted himself. Scoring *Jerusalem* was a job of work for him and is not considered one of his major creations in the same way that his symphonies, chamber music or operatic works are.

Although he could be very dismissive of the English music establishment, Elgar knew and respected Parry. Their paths would often cross and in 1891 the older Parry had even conducted the younger Elgar, who was making a living by playing the violin in an orchestra at Worcester. Parry came to conduct his own choral work *Judith* and Elgar cheekily left his baton on the conductor's stand, later claiming that Parry had used and even bruised it.[14] Both composers moved to Sussex and their homes were within twenty miles of each other when they worked on their musical settings of *Jerusalem*. Parry and his family were in their comfortable house on the coast in Rustington, where Millicent Fawcett visited him and persuaded him to transfer the rights of the song to the suffrage movement while Elgar lived in Brinkwells, a cottage on the South Downs near the village of Fittleworth.

It was at Brinkwells that Elgar, always a keen smoker, recovered from an operation on his throat which involved removing his tonsils, a difficult and painful process for a man in his sixties. Here too he chopped wood, entertained friends and was inspired by the woodlands around him into a late period of creativity. Although he never left the Roman Catholic church, Elgar became more sceptical as he grew older and told his doctor on this deathbed that he had no belief in an afterlife.[15] He developed an almost pantheistic attitude to nature and said of the area around his isolated cottage, "the trees are singing my music".[16] Inspired by the Sussex woodlands, Elgar, like Beethoven, wrote chamber music as a swansong near the end of his life.

After his wife Alice died in 1920, silence descended on the composer and he wrote little of note in the years of widowhood. He remained active in music, however, and both conducted and recorded music. Two years before his death, he met the fifteen-year-old violinist Yehudi Menuhin with whom he recorded his Violin Concerto at Abbey Road, a legendary recording that is still available. It had first been written over twenty years earlier and Menuhin was a late stand-in to play the violin at the recording. There was an age difference of nearly sixty years between the composer and musician but Elgar took a shine to the young prodigy and later wrote a dedication to him on the sheet music of the concerto after he had flown to Paris to conduct Menuhin playing it. This was one of Elgar's last public appearances. Menuhin, for his part, remembered him supervising a rehearsal of the orchestra at Abbey Road and, satisfied that they knew their stuff, going off to enjoy the rest of the day at the races.[17]

Rudyard Kipling was another Sussex writer who lived not far away at Bateman's, a grand house which his daughter later gave to the National Trust in his memory. There is no record of

Kipling bringing his Rolls Royce over from Batemans to visit the Elgars at their modest cottage, but Elgar did set Kipling's seafaring poems *Fringes of the Fleet* to music. He conducted the orchestra himself in a series of popular performances in theatres around the country until Kipling suddenly withdrew his permission. News of the death of his only son John had arrived and Kipling may well have thought that places of light entertainment were no longer suitable venues for his works.[18] Although he put a stop to Elgar conducting these versions of his poems – and earned the enmity of Lady Elgar in the process – the composer did agree to set Kipling's poem *Big Steamers* to music in June 1918. The government asked him to do so and he agreed, saying "anything for the cause", according to Lady Elgar's diary.[19]

"The cause" was support for British troops fighting in the trenches. At first, Elgar had seemed more concerned about the death of animals than of men, exclaiming "Oh, my horses!" when he found out how many had been killed. But, as the war dragged on, the human losses mounted. Nearly twenty thousand soldiers were killed in the first day's fighting at the Battle of the Somme on 1 July 1916, the highest number of deaths in the history of the British army. While his setting of *Jerusalem* had been sung for the first time just three months earlier, Parry was becoming increasingly disillusioned with the war and this led him to switch the rights to the song to the cause of women's suffrage. Kipling meanwhile retreated into private grief. Only Elgar remained an unwavering supporter of the cause and it is his version of *Jerusalem* that is played most often today.

Notes

1. bankofengland.co.uk
2. *Edward Elgar: A Creative Life* by Jerold Northrop Moore (page 102). Even after he was well-established and successful, Elgar constantly worried about money.

3. From *Christmas: 1924* by Thomas Hardy

4. From Boosey and Hawkes website (publishers of *Pomp and Circumstance*) boosey.com/shop/prod/Elgar-Edward-Pomp-Circumstance-March-No-1-Op-39-arr-military-band-set-of-parts/604226

5. Moore (page 247)

6. Ibid (page 364 footnote)

7. *Royal Heritage:* by Huw Wheldon, BBC Programme and Book, Episode Nine

8. This well-known remark can be found in several places, including: elgarsociety.co.uk/wp-content/uploads/2014/04/Pomp-and-Circumstance.-An-Introduction..pdf.

9. Moore (page 357/8)

10. theartsdesk.com/new-music/10-questions-composer-errollyn-wallen

11. Dibble (page 484)

12. Letters of Ralph Vaughan Williams 1895-1958; edited by Hugh Cobbe (Oxford: Oxford University Press, 2008), page 425. Quoted by Keri Davies in an essay entitled *Blake Set to Music*. See keridavies.blogspot.com for more of her views on Blake.

13. bbc.co.uk/news/uk-england-11411360

14. Moore (page 156)

15. Ibid. (page 818)

16. *Elgar, Vicat Cole and the Ghosts of Brinkwells* by Carol Fitzgerald and Brian W Harvey (chapter eight). There is much on Elgar's love of Brinkwells and his relationship with the surrounding woodlands in this book.

17. Moore (page 799)

18. Ibid (page 713)

19. Ibid

Chapter 7

An Anthem for Promenaders

At nine o'clock in the evening of Saturday 16 September 1967, Sir Malcolm Sargent made the short journey from his flat to the Albert Hall for his final public appearance. It was barely a hundred paces from the Albert Hall Mansions across to the scene of so many of his triumphant performances but he was too ill to walk the short distance and needed a car to take him. Even that journey was a strain on a body riven by cancer and he was sick on the way. He had barely eaten for two weeks and even sipping water was painful. Yet Sargent was determined to make the journey and appear on the podium. Nothing would stop the audience's favourite conductor from appearing at his last Last Night of the Proms.[1]

Once he entered the Royal Albert Hall, however, adrenaline took over and Sargent was able to walk unaided to appear at the conductor's rostrum as he had done for almost twenty years. After he had been introduced by his successor as Conductor in Chief Sir Colin Davis, the audience reacted to his surprise appearance with predictable cheers and applause. Sargent was their darling and he knew how to play them as well as any instrument. He said that he intended to make a short speech, adding his own "Hear! Hear!" for good measure before, he said, anyone else had a chance to do so. In what turned out to be his valedictory performance he bravely told the adoring promenaders that the next season would start on 20 July the following year and that, God willing, he would see them then back in the hall.

But God was not willing and Sir Malcolm Sargent died two weeks later. At his last appearance he had worn one of his immaculate suits, with a trademark carnation in his buttonhole, but his clothes had been altered to accommodate a shrivelled frame. His impeccable appearance and assured manner could not disguise the fact that Sargent was a dying man. It was fitting that he should appear in public at this final Last Night of the Proms because this was where he was most loved. A divorced man, who had never found a lifelong companion, whose daughter had died of polio and whose son he had an uneasy relationship with, Sargent felt most loved when he was in front of an adoring audience. To a large extent, he had invented the Last Night as we know it and it was he who had made *Jerusalem* an irreplaceable part of this most British of evenings.

Sargent had not started the Proms, nor had he brought them to the Albert Hall, the venue now most closely associated with this series of summer concerts which are held every year in the heart of London. The very word "promenade" gives away the French origin of this type of concert.[2] It means "walk" and the audience was allowed to walk around while the music was playing. This is still a privilege allowed to the promenaders, often referred to as "prommers". Promenading was meant to encourage the social aspect of the performances but was hardly inclined to heighten the musical appreciation of the pieces being performed.

Early audience members were allowed to smoke as well as to walk while the music was being played, a permission unthinkable today. An advertisement for the 1911 Proms specifically promises "SMOKING PERMITTED" in unmissable capital letters, while non-smokers are reassured (in lower case lettering) that they will have a "portion" of the Grand Circle reserved for their use and preference.[3] Another early advertisement promises that a cigar stall will be provided for customers together with a flower stall and an ice stall, presumably for female concert-goers, while their menfolk are free to puff away.[4]

These early Promenade Concerts took place from 1895 onwards at the newly opened Queen's Hall, Upper Portland

Street, opposite where the BBC headquarters now stands. The Queen's Hall is also the venue where *Jerusalem* was sung in public with Parry's music for the first time at the Fight for Right concert of 1916. That was a more sombre occasion and not one with the light-hearted, almost frivolous atmosphere associated with the Proms. These concerts had been started by Robert Newman, an entrepreneur and music-lover who asked Henry Wood, an up and coming young conductor, to choose the music and conduct the orchestra. Newman was manager of the Queen's Hall and Wood recalled that his aim was to introduce the British public to new music by, "interweaving novelties with the classics".[5]

Prices were to be affordable with the tickets for promenaders costing a shilling (five pence) each or a guinea (a pound and five pence) for a season ticket. Even though the concerts were popular and successful amongst Londoners, money was a constant problem for Newman who went bankrupt in 1902. Edgar Speyer, a wealthy banker and music-lover, then agreed to back the Proms to the tune of £2,000. In gratitude for saving the Proms, the British drove Speyer out of the country during the First World War because of his German connections and he moved with his family to New York.

Although it did not exist as a unified nation until nearly a quarter of a century before the Proms began, Germany has long had a tradition of producing great composers of classical music. This was inevitably reflected in the programme choices for the Proms, which has a justified reputation for being unafraid to introduce new and contemporary work to the audience as a way of educating them. Wagner was by far the most performed composer in the first two decades of the Proms with 2,383 performances of his work at the Queen's Hall, while Beethoven was a distant second with 681 performances. Sullivan, almost forgotten as a serious composer now, was the top Brit with 508 performances, followed by Elgar with 208. Parry is not in this early version of the top twenty, the only other British composer being Charles Villiers Stanford, featured in 63 concerts.[6]

Henry Wood saw to it that popular anti-German sentiment, which caused even the royal family to change their name, did not prevent German music from being played at the Proms during and after the First World War. England, in the dismissive words of the German critic Adolf Schmitt, was "das land ohne musik" – the land without music.[7] Wood and Newman made sure that, even if Britain did not produce much original music, it could still lead the world in performing it. In the same way, Britain does not produce many Grand Slam-winning tennis players but does manage to run the world's most popular tennis tournament every summer at Wimbledon. We may not make many champions but we know how to throw a good party.

A good party is what the Last Night of the Proms became increasingly about. In the early days of the Proms under Henry Wood and Robert Newman, the last night only commanded lower case letters (like the non-smokers) and was exactly that – the final concert in the series, usually held in October when the season came to an end. Henry Wood may have been a commanding presence in front of an orchestra but he preferred conducting to talking and did not make a speech from the rostrum until 1941, three years before his death, when he briefly thanked the sponsors. Even then he left out the name of the season's main backer, Sir Keith Douglas, with whom he had fallen out. Not for nothing did Wood gain the nickname "Old Timber", a reference both to his family name and his character.

Malcolm Sargent, on the other hand, had the dubious honour of being nicknamed "Flash Harry". He did not take over from Wood immediately on the death of the first Prom conductor as he had to wait while Sir Adrian Boult was given the job. Boult, however, did not care for the frivolous and under-rehearsed nature of the Promenade Concerts and was desperate to offload the job to Sargent, a man he heartily despised.[8] Sargent was a well-known figure who had already made his name on BBC radio in *The Brains Trust* where his easy and accessible speaking manner brought him great popularity with the British public. Like Elgar and Blake, Sargent came from a modest background and had moved up in the musical world through talent and hard work. He and Elgar met in 1922 when Sargent had conducted *The Dream of Gerontius* and Elgar took a shine to this ambitious young man from a similar background. Elgar even proposed Sargent for membership of the Beefsteak Club, still an important dining venue and watering hole for creative types in London.[9]

Sargent drove himself very hard and was a demanding leader of an orchestra, so he was not always popular amongst the musicians as a result. He was very successful as a conductor of choral works, however, and much loved by members of the choirs he conducted. He was also very popular with the British people. Sargent was aware that they do not have much patience with a long-winded speech-maker who enjoys the sound of his own voice but that they usually appreciate an eloquent and concise address, preferably with a few jokes thrown in. Wood had allowed the music to do his talking and remained silent at the rostrum until his final years at the Proms when he said a few brief words. In contrast, Sargent took to addressing the promenaders on the Last Night and they enjoyed his teasing, witty speeches. Not only was Sargent well known in Britain from his frequent radio appearances but he had chosen to return to Britain after war was declared with Germany once again in 1939. Sargent had been conducting in Australia at the time and had been offered a lucrative position there but, unlike W H Auden, he chose to make the difficult journey back to Britain and continued to conduct during the war years. He led what was called the "Blitz Tour" through British cities and never allowed an air raid to stop a concert. Sargent, like Wood, also never allowed enmity between Britain and Germany to influence his choice of music. On one occasion when the bombs were dropping, Sargent told the audience that they could leave if they wished to but he would continue to conduct "something that Hitler could never kill", Beethoven's Seventh Symphony. The entire audience remained seated.[10]

British people do not forget that sort of stiff upper lip behaviour, which is often described with the French phrase *sang froid*. When they let their hair down, however, the British are perfectly capable of enjoying themselves and no party goes quite like the Last Night of the Proms. As we now know it, the Last Night was largely the creation of Sir Malcolm Sargent who knew how to turn a concert into an occasion.

While the Last Night at the Albert Hall is now counted as a "traditional" occasion, it had its roots in another event. This was the opening concert at the Royal Festival Hall on 3 May 1951 when Sargent conducted some patriotic songs in the presence of King George VI, his daughter Princess (later Queen) Elizabeth, Prime Minister Clement Atlee, who had laid the foundation stone of the hall two years earlier, and the Archbishop of Canterbury. The previous year Sargent had conducted the band of the Royal Marines in Portsmouth and three years earlier he had been conductor of the orchestra at the opening of the 1948 Olympics in London, so he was used to being in charge at great patriotic and public musical events. He chose for the Festival Hall concert popular tunes like *Land of Hope and Glory*, *Rule Britannia* and *Jerusalem*, which he thought would resonate with the audience. They, in turn, were predictably enthusiastic and the King, who shared his father's conservative musical tastes, said that he had never been so moved by any music. Sir Adrian Boult was visibly uncomfortable in having to follow such rapturously received works with an altogether more serious piece, giving him even more reason to dislike Sargent.[11]

"Flash Harry" had chosen well for his audience in 1951 and he remembered these choices when he came to conduct the Last Night in 1953. When the Proms began in 1895, *Jerusalem* did not exist in musical form. It had been composed as a poem by William Blake a hundred and fifty years before it was first sung at the event with which it is now most associated.

Likewise, *Land of Hope and Glory* had not been composed either musically or lyrically and Henry Wood only created his *Fantasia on British Sea Songs* in 1905 when it was first performed as a tribute to the British Navy on the centenary of the Battle of Trafalgar. Only *Rule Britannia*, composed by Thomas Arne in 1740, was in existence when the Proms began. Far from being a long-established tradition, the Last Night programme did not emerge until the Proms were well over fifty years old and nearly halfway through their history.

The Last Night extravaganza was devised after Sargent who, aware that British concert-goers like to both celebrate their patriotism and sing along noisily, imported the tunes which had been so enthusiastically received across town at the Festival Hall. He had no hesitation in pandering to the tastes of his audience and correctly predicted that these works would soon become favourites. In fact, any attempt to remove them is greeted with fury by promenader traditionalists. They like to dress up in patriotic costumes, wave flags and join in the singing – even the stamping when it comes to Henry Wood's *Fantasia* compilation. The first half of the Last Night programme is changeable every year with a mixture of well-known works and new ones, some making their debut public performance. The second half, however, always features *Land of Hope and Glory,* followed by Wood's *Fantasia* which segues into *Rule Britannia* and is then followed by *Jerusalem* while the audience join in the singing as they wave their flags – even if they are not all English crosses of Saint George or union flags.

The whole event is televised by the BBC with the fidelity and respect they show towards the Queen's Christmas message and the FA Cup Final. The changeable first half is shown on BBC2 and the immutable second half is broadcast on BBC1 – and invariably commands far higher viewing figures as television watchers turn on their sets to join in the party more than to listen respectfully to the music.

The Proms career of Sir Malcolm Sargent is intimately tied up with the BBC's coverage of these concerts, which began not long after he first appeared at the Proms. This was at the Queen's Hall in 1921 when he conducted his own work *Impressions on a Rainy Day*.[12] He later conducted the final concert at a Queen's Hall matinee, just a few hours before it was destroyed by bombing in 1941. By this time the BBC had been broadcasting radio concerts from the Proms for fourteen years, Lord Reith, the corporation's first director considering it part of the BBC's remit to bring classical music to the British people. Every concert at the Proms is now broadcast on Radio Three.

In 1947, twenty years after the first radio broadcast, the BBC showed the Proms on television for the first time. Most people identify the coronation of Elizabeth the Second in 1953 as the event that established television in Britain, but the BBC broadcast the Last Night for the first time six years earlier. By this time the Proms were being performed at the Albert Hall where prommers could sit or even lie on the floor to listen to the music in an improvised manner. The first live broadcast also had an air of improvisation about it. Only two cameras were used and one of these had to be rushed over from the Oval cricket ground where it had been televising a match earlier in the day.[13] In contrast, fifteen cameras and eight vehicles are now needed to broadcast the Last Night.[14]

Unlike his predecessor Sir Adrian Boult and his successor Sir Colin Davis, Sir Malcolm Sargent was a natural television personality. Always impeccably dressed, he knew how to work a room like a skilful politician, aware of the television camera but never forgetting the audience. He was willing to introduce new music to the Proms but was sceptical about the value of using them to educate the public in works that many of them found impenetrable. He was not a fan of pop music or rock and roll and would probably have been horrified at the way whole Proms are now given over to artists like Nina Simone and Stephen Sondheim. "If it ain't broke, don't fix it" could have been his motto for the Last Night festivities.

In this, he differed from his bosses at the BBC, who were usually keen to fix the Last Night with innovations and to introduce new ideas. The Controller of Music at the BBC during the 1960s was Sir William Glock, who reputedly said that the one thing which needed changing was tradition. Having previously looked down on the Proms, Glock took personal control of the programme of music soon after he was appointed. Despite their different outlooks the two men, one an elegant autodidact and traditionalist, the other a waspish intellectual and experimenter, enjoyed a cordial relationship. Sargent had already fallen out with several BBC controllers of music and, although he had been appointed Conductor in Chief of the BBC Symphony Orchestra in 1950, he knew that he could not afford to make too many enemies in the Corporation whose support was essential for the survival of the Proms. When private sponsorship had dried up the BBC had stepped into the breach and effectively taken over the concert programme, so much so that they are now called the BBC Proms. Glock was keen to experiment with foreign conductors, particularly Pierre Boulez, of whom he was an admirer, yet he realised that the Last Night as created by Sargent was sacrosanct.

Innovation continues at the Proms. In 1996, the year after the series had celebrated its centenary, the Proms moved outdoors with the introduction of Proms in the Park when proceedings inside the Albert Hall were shown on a large screen by the Albert Memorial. The indoors audience of six thousand sitters and prommers was augmented by 40,000 more in Hyde Park. The outdoors event proved popular with the public without undermining the demand for tickets inside the hall and Proms in the Park has now been extended to other parts of the UK with showings on screens in cities like Belfast, Glasgow, Manchester and Swansea. The outdoors audience wanted to join in the party and would have little interest in pieces such as Harrison Birtwistle's aptly named *Panic*, a free form saxophone concerto which was controversially introduced into the second half of the proceedings in 1995. Instead, well-known and safe personalities such as the late Terry Wogan and Alan Titchmarsh introduced singers like Barry Manilow and Mick Hucknall to entertain the outdoors crowd with their hits. People pay the best part of fifty pounds to sit outside, have a picnic and listen to familiar music before attention switches to proceedings indoors and they can join in singing *Land of Hope and Glory*, *Rule Britannia* and, of course, *Jerusalem*.

Periodically attempts are made to remove familiar pieces of music which are considered overly imperialistic, even racist, from the Last Night and to dispense with the patriotism that is indelibly associated with the event. There is a difference between patriotism and racism, however, between respecting tradition and being bound by it. The Proms are now multicultural as well as multinational, with musicians and audience members of colour and of both genders welcome at the Albert Hall. In 2020, a new version of *Jerusalem* by Errollyn Wallen had its debut performance and was dedicated to the Windrush generation. The BBC has shown itself keen to show its commitment to diversity by ensuring that all new music commissions will be split equally between male and female composers by 2022. Women conductors like Marin Allsop and Dalia Staseveska have now held the baton at the Last Night. Change is coming and the Proms continues to evolve. Some things are untouchable, however, and the enthusiastic singing of *Jerusalem*, a song loved by both traditionalists and innovators and long accepted into the mainstream, is surely one of them.

Notes

1. *Tunes of Glory* by Richard Aldous (pages 240 - 45). The last chapter of Aldous's biography of Sargent includes a description of the conductor's final appearance at the Albert Hall and his death soon afterwards.

2. Information from David Cannadine's essay *The Last Night of the Proms in Historical Perspective* available to read in the Wiley Online Library: onlinelibrary.wiley.com/doi/ full/10.1111/j.1468-2281.2008.00466.x

3. *The Proms: A New History* by various authors, edited by Jenny Doctor and David Wright (page 53)

4. Ibid (page 54)

5. Ibid (page 97)

6. Ibid (page 62)

7. This terse dismissal received a counterblast from no less a figure than Boris Johnson writing in defence of British composers in a column he wrote for *The Daily Telegraph* on 19 October 2006, long before he became Prime Minister.

8. Aldous (page 142)

9. Ibid. (page 124)

10. Ibid. (page 106)

11. Cannadine essay

12. *The Proms: A New History* (page 109)

13. Ibid (pages 152 – 3)

14. nepgroup.co.uk/project/bbc-proms

Chapter 8

Journey to Jerusalem

If you are lucky enough to have a tour of Westminster Abbey with a London blue badge guide you will enter the abbey through a door on the south side of the nave. You avoid the long queues of people who have to wait to buy their entry tickets at the north door and who are given an audio machine to listen to their commentary. (Those on a guided tour also have the advantage of being able to use the toilets on their way into the abbey via the cloisters, no small advantage for tourists, who always need to pee.) As people on a tour approach Britain's royal church – not a cathedral but a "royal peculiar", as it is known – they show their ticket to a marshal standing in a red cloak by the cloisters. If they take a moment to look beyond the marshal they will see a building called the Jerusalem Chamber. This building, which is not open to visitors, was built nearly six hundred years ago and still belongs to the abbey. It is where a committee established by James I agreed the text of the Authorised Version of the Bible in 1611 and where later versions were also updated and finalised. The Jerusalem Chamber was once part of the Abbot's House when the church was still in use as an abbey. Following the dissolution of the monasteries in the early sixteenth century, it became part of the deanery and is now used by the abbey's dean and chapter.[1]

It is also where one of the most famous death scenes in English history took place, that of King Henry IV in 1413. Or, at least, it took place in the version of English history as imagined by William Shakespeare. Many English people learned the history of their country through the plays of Shakespeare and, although he is not thought of as being a particularly accurate historian these days, most of us have long since forgiven him for not letting the truth get in the way of a good story. He had an audience to entertain, after all, and he also had to stay on the right side of royalty, who could be notoriously prickly when it came to how these stories were told. The House of Tudor won the right to sit on the throne when Henry VII defeated Richard III at Bosworth Field in 1485 and, in spite (maybe because) of being descended from a man who had won the crown in a battle rather through inheritance, Queen Elizabeth I did not like being reminded of the fact that she may have had a pretty slender right to wear it.

In 1601, towards the end of Elizabeth's life, Shakespeare's company put on a performance of *Richard the Second* at the Globe Theatre at the behest of the supporters of the Earl of Essex who paid forty shillings (two pounds) above the normal rate for them to do so.[2] What had probably seemed like a nice little earner turned into a dangerous flirting with rebellion when those same supporters of the Earl led a revolt against the Queen's government the very next day. The players escaped punishment but quickly learned that it was not wise to stage a play about deposing a monarch shortly before an attempt was made to do just that. The Earl and his supporters claimed that it was not Queen Elizabeth herself they were trying to overthrow, but her treacherous advisers.

No dice. Essex paid with his head for his insubordination, not least because he burst into the Queen's chamber unannounced to confront her. Few women, particularly if they are in their late sixties, like to be disturbed before they are ready to face the world, and Essex had gone too far. Putting up the money for a play about insubordination was one thing. Confronting the notoriously vain Elizabeth before she had put on her face was quite another. Do not believe those stories about the Essex ring and the Queen being heartbroken by the execution of her favourite. Look at Essex's death warrant with Elizabeth's bold and decisive signature on it.[3] This is not the writing of a woman unable to make up her mind but of one determined to hold onto her throne. Only death could uncrown her, as it did soon afterwards.

Two centuries earlier, Richard II had been uncrowned by the man who died in the Jerusalem Chamber. Henry Bolingbroke, eldest son of John of Gaunt, had been banished by King Richard in a fit of pique and took his revenge by returning to England in 1399 to seize the throne. His father had died shortly beforehand and Henry would have inherited his considerable estates in Lancaster if Richard had not prevented him from doing so. Richard humiliated but did not destroy Henry Bolingbroke and, with little left to lose, Henry returned to England and easily usurped the unpopular, ineffectual and – important in medieval England where an heir could carry on the line – childless Richard. While Richard had allowed Henry to survive and to lick his wounds, Henry showed no such weakness towards Richard. In Shakespeare's play, the deposed king is murdered. In real life, his body was displayed at Saint Paul's Cathedral to demonstrate that he had not died a bloody death. He probably starved to death, possibly giving up the will to live without his precious crown.

History was repeated nearly a century later when another Henry usurped a later Richard in 1485. This was when Henry Tudor defeated Richard III at the Battle of Bosworth to win the crown and become King Henry VII. You can see Richard's new tomb inside Leicester Cathedral, the nearest one to the battlefield and a statue of him trying to hold onto his crown just outside. The defeated king's bones were recovered in a nearby car park and identified by DNA analysis in 2012.[4] There have been attempts by his supporters – known as Ricardians – to portray Richard as an unjustly deposed and unfairly vilified hero, but most of us prefer to see him as a Shakespearean tyrant. *Richard III* is said to be Shakespeare's most performed play and a nasty villain, such as the one portrayed by Laurence Olivier in the film version, is always more entertaining than a soppy hero. Shakespeare was more or less obliged to portray Richard III as evil personified because the man who took the crown from him at Bosworth was the grandfather of his queen. Henry was the king who brought peace to England after the bloody chaos of the Wars of the Roses. This conflict had started with one Henry seizing the crown from a king called Richard and ended when another Henry was to rid England of a later Richard. The earlier Richard is an ineffectual dreamer, the later one a nasty – if entertaining – villain. While Henry VII disappears from Shakespeare after winning the crown at Bosworth, Henry IV is shown having a troubled guilt-ridden fourteen years on the throne until his death in 1413.

The cause of much of the earlier Henry's troubles was his eldest son, Prince Hal, or Harry of Monmouth, as he was sometimes known, after the town in Wales where he was born. The story of Hal's adventures with Sir John Falstaff – and of the newly crowned king's rejection of his old drinking pal – is well known, although almost entirely invented by Shakespeare. Nor is there any evidence that the prince was present when his father lay dying and the two were reconciled as the older Henry finds the strength to give his wayward son a stern lecture. During this talking-to, he advises him to "seek out foreign quarrels" as a way of uniting the country behind him and warding off the rebellions which had plagued the reign which was about to come to an end when the king dies soon afterwards.

Finally, after giving his son a pep talk and being reconciled with him, King Henry asks what the name of the room is where he has been taken following his collapse and, on being told that it is called the Jerusalem Chamber, he realises that his time is up. He knew that there had been an ancient prophesy that he would die "in Jerusalem" and, thinking this meant he would end his life in a crusade to the Holy Land, had long planned one, only to find that affairs of state prevented him from going there. He had not travelled to Jerusalem as planned but Jerusalem had been on his doorstep all along and now he was to die there.

This part of the story is based on fact. Henry IV did die in the Jerusalem Chamber of Westminster Abbey, having suffered what was probably a stroke while parliament was sitting. His son, moreover, took his dying father's advice (or Shakespeare's version of it, at least) and went on to defeat the French at the Battle of Agincourt two years later in 1415. It was the culmination of a campaign that was both glorious and dubious, glorious in the way an outnumbered hungry and wet English army defeated a larger French one, dubious in that they had precious little right to be there in the first place, the excuses the king made for waging war depending on a ludicrously complicated justification given by the Archbishop of Canterbury who conveniently forgot – or simply ignored – the Fifth Commandment.

Sir John Falstaff is shunted aside ruthlessly by Shakespeare's newly crowned Henry V with that famous line: "I know thee not, old man". Falstaff was one of the playwright's best-loved creations and portraying him is seen as a career milestone for many famous actors, from Anthony Sher (who donned a fat-suit to bulk out his slender frame) to Orson Welles in his film *Chimes at Midnight*. Welles did not need to add to his bulk to portray the self-indulgent survivor Falstaff, a survivor at least until his rejection by King Henry V. In a recent film adaptation of the story, *The King*, Henry is portrayed by the American-French actor Timothee Chalamet and Falstaff by an Australian, Joel Edgerton. In this version, the king and his companion maintain their friendship and Falstaff helps to win the Battle of Agincourt. The film puts a modern slant on the story, keeping many of Shakespeare's characters, while jettisoning his language and that infamous unfriending at the end.

Henry V, in both Shakespeare and history, is a conquering king who goes to war in order to unite his country behind him. He is a Younghusband hero, rather than a Blakeian visionary.

In reality, it was bows rather than bravery that won the day and gave Henry the right to sit on the French throne as well as the English one. The English longbow was the medieval machine gun, capable of firing a dozen times a minute for a longer distance and more rapidly than the French crossbow.[5] The French naively, as they had done in previous battles in the notoriously named Hundred Years' War, expected to win the day at Agincourt with hand to hand fighting between well-armed and armoured knights. Instead, many of them were cut down by an estimated thousand arrows a second, their feathered ends making the ground look like it was covered in snow after they had landed.[6] It was not until the teenaged Joan of Arc came onto the scene after Agincourt that the French finally expelled the invading English from their country.

Six hundred years after Henry had won his famous victory in France, another British army was embedded in a foreign quarrel there while people at home were singing Blake's words to Parry's music as a way of keeping up their spirits. Blake had spent a significant part of his apprenticeship going to Westminster Abbey to learn his trade by drawing pictures of the statues and monuments there, while avoiding the annoying attention of boys from the nearby Westminster School. On his way to the abbey, he must have passed the Jerusalem Chamber many times and seen the building where King Henry IV died, after which Henry V came to the throne. The younger Henry is buried in the abbey, while the older Henry was interred at Canterbury Cathedral, near the place where Thomas a Becket was cut down.

For Henry IV, Jerusalem was a physical place where he could atone for his sins by picking a fight with the people who lived there. These were the Moslems who had occupied the city for centuries but were considered usurpers by Christians. From the late eleventh century onwards popes in Rome had promised anyone going on a crusade forgiveness for their sins if they went to free the city where Christ had died from the grip of the heathen. This was a sure route to Heaven for men like Henry IV. He had seized the crown from Richard and was at least indirectly responsible for the death of his predecessor, so he had a lot to make up for.

Henry was not the only king with a guilty conscience. A century earlier, in 1306, Robert the Bruce had killed John Comyn, one of his rivals for the throne of Scotland, inside Greyfriars Church in Dumfries. To kill one of your enemies was not unknown in medieval times, but to do so inside a church in the full view of others was a bit over the top, and Bruce was excommunicated by the pope for his misdeed. This did not delay his coronation at Saint Andrews the following month and the beginning of his long-running war against the English occupiers who were finally and comprehensively defeated at Bannockburn eight years later on midsummer's day in 1314. Bruce was now unchallenged as King of Scots – always of Scots, never of Scotland – but it took another fourteen years for the English monarch to accept him as de facto ruler north of the border.

Robert the Bruce, like Henry IV of England, had always intended to atone for sins like the killing of Comyn by leading a crusade to Jerusalem. However, the need to rebuild a devastated Scotland and make the English recognise him as the rightful ruler of the country had long prevented him from doing so. Eventually, after he died in 1329, his heart was cut out of his corpse and taken by a group of his knights on a crusade led by Sir James Douglas. This tartan army, however, never got close to Jerusalem and most were killed in a battle in Spain fighting against the Moors. Bruce's heart was then brought back to Scotland by the survivors and buried in Melrose Abbey, the rest of him having been interred at Dunfermline.

For medieval kings, Jerusalem was an actual city you went to in order to win a place in Heaven. You guaranteed this by doing what you did best, namely killing lots of your fellow human beings in wars, albeit holy ones. For William Blake, on the other hand, Jerusalem was an ideal city, somewhere that existed only in his imagination. This did not mean that it was any less real for him than the place the crusaders hoped to recapture from the Moslems. For Blake, Jerusalem was found in an ancient England called Albion. While most people are familiar with the sixteen lines which make up the poem we call *Jerusalem*, only dedicated Blake enthusiasts will read the work that he called *Jerusalem* and which is subtitled *The Emanation of the Giant Albion*. This is a long and complex epic poem, one of Blake's Prophetic Books. It is a far more difficult work, Blake's personal vision which he wrote and illustrated. There are ten original versions of this longer *Jerusalem*, six created in his lifetime and four posthumously. Each is slightly different as Blake would alter the text and pictures as he created separate versions of this epic work.

The long poem which Blake called *Jerusalem* was created in the years after 1803 when the Blakes left Sussex to return to live in South Molton Street in London. It tells the story of the fall of Albion and is peopled with characters such as Los and his enemy Vala who spring out of Blake's imagination in his created and often confusing world. However, it is part of the charm of Blake that, amongst these creatures and kingdoms of his imagination, familiar people and places crop up. The Rivers Trent and Thames are mentioned along with many other familiar British landmarks. Our old friend (and Blake's enemy) John Scofield also makes a guest appearance in the work. Several, in fact, as Blake considers "Skofield" (as he spells his name) to be a symbol of all that is wrong with England. This rather absurd soldier, who was bested by the hot-tempered but otherwise harmless artist who lived across the road from him in Felpham, is identified by Los as one of the "Ministers of Evil"[7] in the poem that Blake called *Jerusalem*. Blake's attitude to militarism is encapsulated in his dislike for Scofield, a soldier who had been publicly humiliated by the artist and took his revenge by reporting him to the authorities. Although he was unable to achieve a result through this sneaky act, Scofield had obviously got under the skin of the artist who could never forget their argument even after he had returned to London from Sussex.

Blake used the ancient name Albion to refer to Britain, which is thought to derive from the word for "white". For many Sussex people, however, the Albion is their local soccer club Brighton and Hove Albion and getting a result means staying in the Premier League. The club originally intended to adopt the name Brighton and Hove United until the supporters of a football team in Hove objected to the suggestion that they had been absorbed into a team with the name Brighton. (Residents of Hove actually can be very prickly about such matters.) With the nearby chalk cliffs suggesting whiteness, the team adopted the name of Albion instead and they are one of the few teams who use it. The other well-known club to do so is West Bromwich Albion from Birmingham. They play in a similar blue and white kit and this may have influenced the choice of the name of the Brighton club.[8] Dame Vera Lynn, well known for singing *The White Cliffs of Dover* in the Second World War, lived in Ditchling a few miles from Brighton and Hove Albion's stadium in Falmer until her death in 2020.

While he was working on his longer version of *Jerusalem*, Blake also took on what he hoped would be a more lucrative commission, drawing a picture of the pilgrims who journeyed to Canterbury to pay homage at the tomb of Thomas a Becket. However, his large picture of this motley crew as imagined by Geoffrey Chaucer – including the Knight, the Nun, the Miller and the Wife of Bath – ended up being one of Blake's many financial failures. The artist's onetime friend Robert Hartley Cromek had originally commissioned Blake to do the job but then chose another artist Robert Stothard to portray the pilgrims instead.

Blake did the hard work while Stothard simply copied his version which was sold to the public through an engraving made by an Italian, Luigi Schiavonetti (nicknamed "Assassinetti" by Blake). While the Stothard-Cromek-Schiavonetti work became a great success, Blake's original picture earned him virtually nothing and was exhibited in the one-man show above his brother's shop which proved to be such a failure.[9] Unprotected at the time by concepts such as copyright and intellectual property, Blake could only fume at the injustice of it all.

However, it is William Blake who is remembered in Westminster Abbey today in one of the most striking images found in the church, while those who exploited him are long forgotten. A bust of Blake by Jacob Epstein is attached to a column near the grave of Geoffrey Chaucer, the original creator of the Pilgrims who was buried in the abbey after he had died in 1400. Living nearby and being a servant of the crown, Chaucer was given a grave in the South Transept of the church and the Elizabethan poet Edmund Spenser later asked to be buried near to this father of English poetry. The tradition of poets and writers being buried or commemorated here grew up in what is now called Poet's Corner. You can see the graves of those two great Victorian versifiers Robert Browning and Alfred Tennyson next to each other in front of Chaucer's tomb. Charles Dickens, Rudyard Kipling and Thomas Hardy all lie check by jowl near the grave of George Frederick Handel, neither an Englishman nor a poet, but adopted and loved enough by the British to be buried in the Abbey.

Some writers were unruly types who did not respect the established Church of England when alive and thus disqualified themselves from being buried within the country's major Anglican church. Near to Chaucer, you will see the names but not the tombs of many doubters and disbelievers – from the intellectually sceptical George Eliot (born MaryAnn Evans) to the "mad, bad and dangerous to know" Lord Byron. In our more tolerant and agnostic time they have now been accepted and given memorials, usually stones discreetly placed on the floor. Blake could not be accused of being a doubter or disbeliever, but his religious views did not conform to those of the established church of the day, so it was not until 1957, just a few days short of what would have been his two hundredth birthday, that Epstein's bust was unveiled. Discreet it is not. Blake's passionate nature seems to burn out of the bronze and it shows a very different side to the man portrayed as a competent and mildly successful man of business in the painting by Thomas Phillips. It needed an Epstein, like Blake an outsider, to do justice to his intense and uncompromising personality.[10]

William Blake is the only person apart from Winston Churchill to be memorialised in both Saint Paul's Cathedral and Westminster Abbey, without being buried in either church. He may have been a prophet without honour in his own time, but the words Blake wrote, and which were later purloined by Sir Francis Younghusband's Fight for Right movement, lived on long after those who adopted them have been forgotten. He would not have approved of the foreign quarrel being fought with his unwitting support, but the use of his poem did at least bring back *Jerusalem* into the consciousness of people around the world and our singing it does something to make up for the shoddy treatment and neglect Blake was subject to during his lifetime.

Notes

1. westminster-abbey.org/about-the-abbey/history/jerusalem-chamber#i17235

2. historic-uk.com/HistoryUK/HistoryofEngland/Shakespeare-Richard-II-Rebellion/

3. You can view (and purchase a copy of) the warrant at: alamy.com/stock-photo-a-facsimile-of-queen-elizabeth-is-signature-on-the-death-warrant-of-105362512.html

4. *The King in the Car Park* by Terry Breverton (also a Channel Four documentary)
5. history-magazine.com/longbow
6. Ibid
7. *Jerusalem* (First Chapter, just before Plate 18)
8. For more on the history of the Brighton and Hove football club's name go to: wearebrighton.com/albionfeatures/ where-did-the-name-brighton-hove-albion-come-from/
9. William Blake, Tate Gallery, by Martin Myrone and Amy Concannon (page 143)
10. westminster-abbey.org/abbey-commemorations/William-blake#i2415

Chapter 9

A New Jerusalem

Although it is usually the national government that foots most of the bill, it is always a city rather than a country that is awarded the Olympics. London has received this honour three times, the only city on the planet to do so. The first time was in 1908, for which no accurate records of the costings are available. The second time was in 1948, when the British government stumped up around three-quarters of a million pounds but made some of that back from the taxes levied on tickets sold for the then strictly amateur Olympics. Red double-decker buses were pressed into service for transporting the athletes and former prisoner of war camps used to house them. The cost of "the austerity games", as they were known, was fairly small and the occasion was conducted in an atmosphere that combined light-heartedness and a post-war spirit of can-do and improvisation.

The most recent Olympics to be held in London in 2012, however, were to prove a far more expensive affair. Providing the infrastructure and building the venues needed to stage the events ended up costing somewhere in the region of nine *billion* pounds, well above the original estimate.[1] The costs of actually running the event was free for the taxpayer as these were covered by private money, mostly through sponsorship and ticket sales. Expensive but eventually worthwhile was the general verdict. The Olympics helped to boost national morale and regenerate a run-down part of London as well as providing the capital with a new 60,000 seat stadium. Originally intended as an athletics venue, this proved unviable and the London Stadium, as it is now called, became the home of West Ham United football club, a once homely outfit who played at the friendly but crowded Boleyn Ground at Upton Park and had a reputation for fielding teams full of players who had grown up in the East End of London. These included three men who helped England win their only World Cup in 1966, the captain Bobby Moore and both the other goal scorers, Martin Peters and Geoff Hurst, still the only man to have scored a hat trick in a World Cup Final.

A chunk of that nine billion pounds went to pay for the opening ceremony directed by the filmmaker Danny Boyle. Named *Isles of Wonder*, the ceremony took four hours, cost twenty-seven million pounds (twice the original budget) and, despite scepticism from many people before it began, was considered a great success.[2] It was watched by an audience estimated at nine hundred million people and celebrated both Britain's industrial heritage and its National Health Service. One of the secrets of the event's success was that it did not try too hard to impress purely with spectacle but spiced things up with some typical British humour. Rowan Atkinson spoofed the opening sequence of *Chariots of Fire* by hitching a ride in a car to keep up with the other runners on the beach at Saint Andrew's and even the Queen took part, accompanied by Daniel Craig playing her most famous spy, James Bond. Her Majesty was reportedly quite happy to be involved, although her arrival by parachute from a helicopter together with Bond involved a sleight of hand – and camera.

Unlike in the soccer or rugby World Cups, where the home nations all compete as separate entities, Britain fields a team at the Olympics which consists of athletes from England, Scotland and Wales, those from Northern Ireland having the choice of representing either Ireland or joining what is known as Team GB, presumably on whether their loyalties are republican or unionist. Athletes at the Olympics do not represent their country in quite the same way that players of team sports do in their World Cups. The athletes compete for individual medals while the members of the squad of a team sport work together as eleven or more players to try and win a trophy. If they are victorious they are awarded winner's medals but these are not usually treasured in quite the same way as Olympic medals, which represent the triumph of an individual against his or her opponents.

When members of a victorious side are congratulated after a victory, they usually say something about the success of the team being more important than their individual contribution. There may be an element of humble bragging in this but there is a real sense in which every football, cricket or rugby player knows that he or she is dependent on the efforts of sometimes less glamorous teammates in achieving glory. Olympic athletes, however, rarely feel the need to praise fellow members of Team GB in this way. They all compete in separate disciplines and may have little or no contact with those who perform in other sports. (After the games are over and the parties start is a different matter and "contact" can become quite intimate, not to say lusty.) The medals table, which compares the efforts of different countries in winning medals, is more for national pride than for the satisfaction of athletes, whose success is individual rather than national. The slightly amorphous concept of a British national team, therefore, works better for the Olympics than for team sports. There have been attempts to form a British soccer team but there was never much enthusiasm for the idea. People simply cannot get aroused by the idea of competing for Britain in the same way that they can if they are playing for England, Scotland, Wales or Ireland.

Faced with the delicate task of bringing together the four countries whose athletes make up Team GB in the opening ceremony, Danny Boyle did not try to promote the concept of a united kingdom but used choirs from each home country to sing a song that represented the character, history and tradition of their individual nation. Listed alphabetically, these nations are England, Ireland, Scotland and Wales. They make up an entity which we used to call "the British Isles", although that phrase has gone out of fashion and is rarely found in modern atlases. As Ireland is divided in two, a republican south and a British north, many Irish people – who would never see themselves as in any way British – heartily dislike the phrase. Try going into a Dublin pub and start talking about "the British Isles" and see how long it is before someone pours a pint of Guinness over you – or worse.

Likewise, the British national anthem *God Save the Queen* was conspicuous by its absence at the ceremony, although a punk version sung by the Sex Pistols did make a brief appearance. (The Queen's opinion of this version, like so much else to do with her, is a closely guarded secret.) Some Irish competitors – as well as nationalists from Scotland or Wales – would have been hostile to the idea of singing an anthem wishing long life to a monarch identified with the United Kingdom at the Olympic opening ceremony. To be fair to the Queen, she is half-Scottish as her mother was born near Dundee at Glamis Castle and two of the five royal homes (Balmoral Castle near Aberdeen and Holyrood Palace in Edinburgh) are in Scotland. Nevertheless, the Queen reigns over the whole of the United Kingdom and is irretrievably identified with the idea of union. Boyle wanted to keep those who regard themselves first of all as Irish, Scottish or Welsh (even as English) happy. While not denying or undermining the existence of the United Kingdom or Team GB, the Olympics opening ceremony concentrated more on celebrating the individual identities of England, Scotland, Wales and Ireland. To do this Boyle needed songs that were well known, patriotic and not too identified with the British establishment. This was to be a rock and roll event, not a stuffy one.

Ireland was represented by that old favourite *Danny Boy*. A group of Irish choristers were filmed singing it at the Giant's Causeway in County Antrim, Northern Ireland. Although the song is popular in the Irish Republic and is often identified with the independence movement, it is based on an old folk tune known as *The Londonderry Air*. (Londonderry is Northern Ireland's second-largest city and is about an hour's drive from the Causeway.) Even this name might cause problems with republicans who refer to the city as Derry, leaving off the unionist "London" from its name. You often see road signs in Northern Ireland where the "London" has been covered with spray paint by republicans who do not care for the prefix. However, changing the name of the tune might give rise to double entendres, this French idiom being particularly apt if you were to call it by the name "The Derry Air". In a further irony, the words of this most Irish song were written by an English lawyer, Frederic Weatherall, who reputedly set them to the Irish tune at the suggestion of his sister.

The Welsh contribution was less controversial. A Welsh choir sang *Cwm Rhondda*, often called *Bread of Heaven*, which like *Jerusalem* is an old and reliable song much loved by those who go to church or chapel. As well as being a religious hymn, it is identified with Wales's sporting prowess, particularly on the rugby pitch, and shots of the choir singing at a beach in the Gower Peninsula were interspersed with pieces of action showing the Welsh rugby team winning some of their famous victories. *Cwm Rhondda* is regularly sung by the Welsh crowd to inspire their team to glory. The way that the last lines of each verse ("Feed me till I want no more", "Be thou still my strength and shield" and "I will ever give to thee") are repeated gives the song an extra power, just as the last lines of the verses of that other great hymn *Dear Lord and Father of Mankind* are repeated.

And the Scots? A Scottish choir sang *Flower of Scotland*, a warlike ballad celebrating their victory over the English at Bannockburn. This is another anthemic song belted out by the nation's rugby supporters to inspire their team at their national stadium, Murrayfield in Edinburgh. Scotland defines itself as much by its anti-English attitude as anything else, so it was somehow inevitable that the defeat of "proud Edward's army" on midsummer's day in 1314 should become their unofficial national anthem, even if singing it lustily at Edinburgh Castle did tend to undermine the partnership between the nations which made up Team GB.

While a different song might have been chosen for Scotland, there was little competition for *Jerusalem* as a specifically English anthem. Blake's poem does not celebrate a military victory – although it does refer to "mental fight" and four different weapons appear in the words: "bow of burning gold", "arrows of desire" and a spear and sword with which he intends to build the new Jerusalem. Glastonbury Tor, where the legend began, was recreated on a manmade hill in the Olympic Stadium and this was cleverly lifted up to allow the arrival of smokestacks and beam engines arising from underneath. Participants dressed in costume marched around as the furnaces blazed away. This was a celebration of what had been achieved through the workings of those dark satanic mills as well as of the beauty of our green and pleasant landscape.

Most people consider the 2012 London Olympics a success that led not only to the building of a new stadium but also to the new Queen Elizabeth Olympic Park straddling the River Lea. The Lea traditionally marked the eastern boundary of London, although the capital has long since sprawled beyond it. It was to the east end of the city that the smelly and toxic industries were sent when London was an industrial as well as a commercial centre. The reason is simply that the prevailing wind in Britain comes from the west so bad smells could be blown away from the delicate noses of the fashionable elite who lived in the more expensive western suburbs. Tanneries, distilleries, soap factories and other nausea-inducing workplaces were encouraged eastwards and property prices were correspondingly lower in this part of London. The east end was also disproportionately damaged by bombing during the Second World War as the eastern part of the city was on the way to and from Germany. While the first London Olympics was held in the western part of the city and the second was in the north, the east end was chosen for the third as much as a way of regenerating the area as of acknowledging the sporting tradition it held, one that has produced athletes like Daley Thompson and Christine Ohuruogu. In turn, the east end benefited from the investment made in the area by staging the games there. The figure usually given by supporters of the Olympics project is that three-quarters of the money used to build the infrastructure of the games remained in the area afterwards. Not only was the London Stadium created but so too was an Aquatics Centre that combined both a revolutionary piece of architecture and a practical swimming pool designed by the late Zahar Hadid. The Copper Box stadium and the Velodrome survived after the games while the venue used for basketball – never a big sport in Britain – was taken down. Housing and office spaces, as well as parkland and gardens, have grown up and most people enjoyed watching the athletes competing, even if they were not too happy about the traffic privileges they were granted.

Moreover, as a nation we are now are both more interested in and more successful at achieving high rankings in the Olympics medals table than we used to be. In the 1996 summer Olympics Team GB ranked thirty-sixth in the table. This was admittedly a bad year, as Britain usually hovered around tenth to twelfth in the rankings. By 2012, however, Team GB had moved up to third and, by the end of the 2016 games in Rio de Janeiro, it was up to the giddy heights of second, above China but still below the USA.

Not everyone, however, was happy with the London Olympics. The writer Iain Sinclair can usually be relied on to bring his grumpy brand of controversialism to bear in such situations and he claimed that the 2012 Games "ruined my patch of London".[3] Unsurprisingly, Sinclair is not a fan of *Jerusalem* either – or, at least, not of the way Blake's poem has been appropriated in the cause of patriotism by being sung at great national festivals. He has said that "Blake declines into a heritage token to be bolted onto the bonnet of any old banger".[4]

That is a good phrase, using old-fashioned English alliteration to make its point, but it should not be taken as a dismissal of Blake as an artist or writer. In fact, you have the feeling that Iain Sinclair and William Blake might have got along famously. They were certainly cut from the same cloth: both Londoners through and through, both outsiders, radicals, visionaries. Neither Sinclair nor Blake cared much for being on the best-seller lists or for amassing worldly wealth if it meant sacrificing their principles. Neither are jumpers on bandwagons or joiners of popular causes. You would not think of either Blake or Sinclair as being supporters of unthinking patriotism, whether it is of an English or a British type.

Jerusalem is sung by people expressing a particularly English type of patriotism. They are not celebrating the whole of the United Kingdom, but their part of it. At the time of writing England has a population of over fifty-six million, while the rest of the UK as a whole musters just ten and a half million people.[5] This means that there are more than five times as many people living in England as there are in Scotland, Wales and Northern Ireland put together. It has to be conceded that some of those fifty-six million would not classify themselves as English but as Celtic exiles who had to cross the border to make a living. Yet the English still outnumber their neighbours, with whom they are bound in an increasingly fragile union. Englishness and Britishness are often confused, to the annoyance of people who regard themselves as British but not English. The smaller nations in the UK embrace their underdog status and relish being able to put one over the arrogant English, originally on the battlefield, now on the sports field. The English, meanwhile, are unable to feel like underdogs and are embarrassed by their numerical superiority and the assumption – which they usually do not share – that they have it in for their neighbours. Singing *Jerusalem* is a rare opportunity for them to celebrate an English identity above a British one.

It is on the sports field that this identity is expressed most fiercely. Polite applause might greet the success of Team GB but raucous cheers accompany a victory by teams from England, Scotland, Wales or Ireland, North or South. Ireland has a united team for rugby union but separate ones represent Northern Ireland and the Republic at soccer, not because rugby is a hotbed of republicanism, but rather because rugby players do not worry about such matters as the historic division of the country, while followers of soccer, particularly those in Northern Ireland, seem to think it is important enough to justify separate teams, even if that decreases their chance of glory. To add to the irony, the only time a Southern Irish team has approached major success in a tournament in recent years was under the managership of an Englishman, the late Jack Charlton. He and his brother Bobby had been members of England's victorious team in the 1966 World Cup. The Irish team he coached had the character of his dour defending rather than his brother's more spectacular attacking qualities.

The fans of sports teams usually like to celebrate the success of their sides with suitable anthems. Sometimes these are imposed from above, sometimes developed from below. Supporters of the Irish soccer and rugby teams have both taken to singing *The Fields of Athenry* during matches to express their support for the team in green. Pete St John's ballad about the potato famine in Ireland during the nineteenth century is a catchy song and celebrates the underdog status of an Irish people oppressed by the Anglo-Saxon outsider so it fits the bill nicely for Irish fans and is also sung by the fans of the Celtic soccer team which has strong links with Southern Ireland and whose supporters tend to be Roman Catholic, while those of their Glasgow rivals Rangers are far more likely to be Protestant.

The Fields of Athenry is a bottom-up anthem, chosen by the fans because it reflects the character of the team, the fans and the country they come from. English rugby fans, lacking a song of their own that promoted an outsider or underdog status, chose instead to sing *Swing Low, Sweet Chariot*, originally a song written by a freed slave called Wallis Willis and often associated with the civil rights movement in the USA. While rugby fans have never been particularly associated with either civil rights or slavery, the game has given opportunities to many black players in recent years and the song was first recorded being sung by supporters at Twickenham Stadium in 1987 when Martin Offiah was playing.[6]

Offiah was a winger and gained the nickname "Chariot" because of his speed over a short distance and the similarity of his name to that of the film *Chariots of Fire* (although it should properly be pronounced "off-ee-ah"). The song gradually became associated with the England rugby team and is regularly sung by the team's supporters. This led to them being accused of cultural appropriation by those who do not like the idea of a slave song being sung by supporters of a sport associated with privilege and which was one of the last to join the sporting boycott of apartheid South Africa. *Swing Low Sweet Chariot*, however, was also banned by the Nazis and, while a few people may wag their fingers, it is unlikely the Rugby Football Union will strenuously try to prevent fans of the England team from singing it.

The other sport which was slow to join the sporting boycott against apartheid was cricket. While English cricket has a notably noisy group of fans – known as "the barmy army" – which has devised ingenious ways to keep its members amused during a five-day test match, this same army has never picked an anthem of its own. They wear outrageous costumes, drink lots of beer and cheer up both the crowd and players during the inevitable slow periods in a long game of cricket. They even have their own website[7] but the barmy army does not have a song of its own in the way that *Swing Low* is associated with England's rugby union fans. *Jerusalem* was chosen from above as an anthem by England's ruling body, the MCC. The song is broadcast before play starts and the army sing it when the team is playing, but its use was ordained more from on high than from below.

This might be because *Jerusalem* is an English song and the England cricket team is anything but, consisting of players shoe-horned in from other countries because of their ability rather than their origin, in much the same way that many of Jack Charlton's Irish team had fairly distant connections with Ireland. Former "England" captains Andrew Strauss and Kevin Pietersen were born in South Africa, Colin Cowdrey and Nasser Hussain in India while Ben Stokes hails from New Zealand. Moreover, Scotland, Ireland and Wales are routinely relieved of their top players to represent England in what is not so much Team GB or Team UK as Team Commonwealth. Yet members of the barmy army still dress up as crusading knights with Saint George's crosses on them, surely the ultimate symbol of English arrogance and exceptionalism.

The contrast between the two types of sporting anthem is seen in the two different versions of rugby played in Britain. Rugby union was strictly amateur for years, while rugby league was developed specifically to allow players to make money from their sporting skills. The game was founded in 1895 as teams in the north of England broke away from the Rugby Football Union, who considered that "if men could not afford to play, then they should not play at all".[8] The amateur code, however, was gradually eroded in the union version of the game, to the extent that most union players now make a better living than those in the increasingly marginalised rugby league world.

Movement between the two codes was originally entirely one way, from union to league, as those bound by amateurism wanted to take advantage of the opportunities to earn money offered by professionalism. Now players are more likely to move towards the greater rewards offered by the once amateur rugby union.

While England's rugby union fans sang *Swing Low Sweet Chariot*, the fans of the other home nations had plenty of songs to choose from and sing *Flower of Scotland, Cwm Rhondda* and *The Fields of Athenry,* unprompted by those who sit in the expensive seats. The men (usually) who run rugby league felt that the sport needed its own anthem in order to offer competition for fans and players presented from the re-invigorated and now professionalised union version of the game. They chose *Jerusalem* which was well known – and cheap, as they did not need to pay royalties or ask anyone permission to use it before games. It was sung by Laura Wright who said that she was "honoured" to be chosen to do so before the Super League Final in 2019 and it is also played before England's international games.

Booking (and presumably paying) a professional singer to perform a song over the public address system before kick-off turns the choosing of a song into a top-down process. *Abide With Me* was introduced to the FA Cup Final a hundred years ago because the Secretary of the Football Association thought that Henry Lyte's hymn would be more dignified than *Alexander's Ragtime Band* and King George V and Queen Mary agreed with him. (The monarch's opinion on such matters counted at the time.) Ever since then the Football Association has had the hymn performed before the Cup Final, led by a professional with the fans joining in, although not many of them know all the words off by heart.[9]

Whatever its merits and popularity *Jerusalem* is always likely to be a top-down anthem imposed from above rather than a people's song growing from below. It is a suitable and safe choice made by men (again, usually) wearing suits and blazers rather than by the fans sporting their team's colours, purchased at the club shop to help pay the players" ever-increasing salaries – or wages, as they are still sometimes quaintly called, as though the players were still members of the working-class with annual incomes in seven or eight digits.

George V was not noted as a soccer fan but was said to be a lover of *Jerusalem* – although it is unlikely that he was all that familiar with other works by William Blake. If the monarch can favour a song whose words were written by a republican supporter of the French Revolution, then William Blake would seem to have lost his hold on it. In truth, that began to happen the moment the audience welled up and sang *Jerusalem* in the Queen's Hall in 1916 at the concert intended to promote Fight for Right during the First World War.

Sport and war have a good deal in common, George Orwell saying that the first was just the same as the second but without the shooting. Both use the same vocabulary of words like sacrifice, heroism and discipline. Both rely on tactics and teamwork with occasional flashes of individual heroism. Both sport and war involve groups of men (and, increasingly, these days, women) putting on uniforms and slugging it out with their opponents until one side achieves victory, at which point the players jump into the bath while the soldiers raise their arms either in triumph or surrender. While football teams are not allowed to publicly endorse political movements in what they wear, football players in the English Premier League, wherever they come from, find that poppies in honour of fallen soldiers are routinely sewn into their kits once a year unless they specifically – and bravely – ask for them to be omitted.

Once it had been purloined as a military song, therefore, it was inevitable that *Jerusalem* would become a sporting anthem as well. This is anathema to many on the left. While most British Labour politicians like to show off their street credibility by ostentatiously supporting a football team, others on the left are suspicious of sport's similarities to militarism and they suspect, often rightly, that repressive governments like to distract people from political problems by achieving and emphasising sporting success. Many people are still convinced that Argentina's emphatic six-nil victory in the 1978 football World Cup – a virtually unknown score in the later stages of the competition – was engineered by the country's military government in order to bring their team to the final (which they won) on home soil and thus both bring some kudos to and guarantee the survival of a borderline fascist regime.

While England was not at that world cup and had no opportunity to sing *Jerusalem* or any other anthem, there is a feeling amongst many left-wingers that Blake's words are not being used for what they were intended when they are sung to encourage worldly success – either on the battlefield or the sports field. They need not despair, however. *Jerusalem* does not belong to any one side in a political battle between left and right and those who see it as the song of a rebellious spirit have found ways of performing it to support their worldview.

Jerusalem was first used as a party political song in 1945 when the Labour Party closed their conference by singing it together en masse. Their leader Clement Atlee had promised that a Labour government would build "a new Jerusalem". Rather than establishing a Blakeain paradise, this involved creating a National Health Service and a welfare state paid for by taxation. It also involved Britain obtaining an atomic bomb and sending soldiers to fight in the Korean war on the American side, which would probably not have gained approval from the man who wrote the words of the song. *Jerusalem* has also been sung at party conferences held by the Liberal and Conservative parties, proving just how versatile it can be. Only the non-English nationalist parties and the Green party have failed to make use of it, although you suspect that a Blake alive today might well align with the greens. The song does, after all, celebrate a "green and pleasant land".

Chris Dann could never be classified as a conservative with a small or capital "c". He works as a musician and has long loved *Jerusalem* both as a poem and a song. He says: "despite it being about 'England' I've never considered it nationalistic. For me 'England' has always been a metaphor for the self and personal transformation, to fight fearlessly and drive forward, to never give up, to become the best we can be and to create Jerusalem in our minds and hearts where there were once dark, satanic mills. I feel similarly about *La Marseillaise*, another amazing and inspiring work that, for me, is about taking up arms and fighting the evil aggressor wherever and whatever that aggressor might be to us, not a narrow-minded nationalistic interpretation."[10] *La Marseillaise* was written shortly before Blake penned the words of *Jerusalem*. If Chris Dann can compare this song of the French Revolution – now the official national anthem of France – with England's hymn, then all is not lost for people on the left who want to reclaim *Jerusalem* for their cause.[11]

One man undoubtedly on the left is Billy Bragg, a self-described "agitator of the 1980s".[12] He has recorded *Jerusalem* several times, most recently as a tribute to the Women's Institute. Bragg has not mellowed with old age and given up his earlier left-wing views under the pressures of parenthood and mortgage payments, as so many others do. Yet he was impressed with the way his local WI in Dorset were making personal protective equipment for National Health Service staff during the coronavirus outbreak and played *Jerusalem* on the guitar in his back garden as a tribute to their efforts. This was thirty years after he first recorded the song on the album *Internationale*. A later album is called William Bloke, an obvious reference to the poet with whom he shares a first name.

Bragg, like Blake, has been trying to reclaim patriotism from the right. The Saint George's flag, more than the Union

Jack or its Celtic equivalents, tends to be associated with right-wing groups such as the English Defence League (EDL), who display it prominently on their marches and demonstrations. The movement's most prominent member was Stephen Yaxley-Lennon, better known by the pseudonym Tommy Robinson, a name he probably adopted in order to conceal the criminal convictions he had obtained while using his real name.

Robinson, as he is generally known, used to be a member of the British National Party (BNP) but says that he left when he found out that it was a racist organisation that did not admit non-white members. He claims that EDL is multiracial, even if it is also anti-Islamic. Being black is acceptable but being a Moslem is not, apparently, if you want to join the EDL.

Bragg and Robinson are at opposite ends of the political spectrum but they also have certain similarities. Both men come from a working class background and were born in towns just outside London where mainly white men would work in dark satanic mills that have now closed. (Bragg is from Barking, Robinson from Luton). Both men developed political philosophies in reaction to the changes taking place where they grew up, one moving to the right, the other to the left. Both men like the English national flag, although Bragg has mixed feelings about the way it is used by those on the right. Both men identify with Jerusalem, Bragg with the song, Robinson with the city, as he is strongly Zionist. He sees this as being tied in with his campaign against the Islamification of Britain.

Britain's right-wing organisations are not particularly identified with any song and *Jerusalem* is probably considered a bit suspect by many who are members of them. *The White Cliffs of Dover* is more their type of tune and, although the BNP has sold a CD that includes it, Dame Vera Lynn refused to allow them to use the song for propaganda purposes or to imply that the "white" in the title is racial rather than geological.[13] She did not own the copyright to the song but was careful to remain strictly neutral on political matters, refusing to endorse any party or product, once even going to court to prevent her name being used to sell gin.[14]

Jerusalem is probably more of a song for the left than for the right even if it has now entered the mainstream. In 2007, a group of public schoolboys reconnected over Facebook and decided to form a singing group, making them probably the first band to be put together via social media. They struggled to find a name until they decided to record *Jerusalem* for their first album and realised that they were all admirers of the poet and painter who had written the words. "It suddenly felt like a natural name for the group," said their spokesman Alex Hopkirk. "Within hours of first discussing it, the name had stuck."[15] Blake sang *Jerusalem* next to their hero's grave and recorded it for a video played on *Songs of Praise*, the BBC's popular hymn programme. In deference to the Christian setting, they add an "Amen" at the end, which is not in the original poem.

A group of clean-cut posh boys singing in a cathedral wearing jackets and ties may not seem particularly radical to Billy Bragg, who favours casual shirts and jeans and is never slow to voice his political opinions. He must be the only singer to have reached number one in the charts who could write a sentence like: "In order to correct the balance of power that produces low unemployment figures yet leaves record numbers of workers stranded below the poverty line, citizens must be given the opportunity to vote for policies that hold the markets to account."[16] Yet, no matter how many times he sings *Jerusalem*, Bragg will never make Blake a conventionally left-wing figure. The poet was just too individual a man to be boxed in by any party political classification.

Jerusalem regularly appears on compilation albums and there are dozens of version of it available to view on YouTube. It is sung by members of the Women's Institute, by crowds at cricket or rugby matches and by individuals playing Parry's tune instrumentally or singing it with Blake's words. A version was recorded by the rock group Emerson, Lake and Palmer which was released as a single but then banned by the BBC. The Fall recorded the song with Mark Smith belting out the words to a drums and electric guitar accompaniment. Bruce Dickinson of Iron Maiden sings his version at Canterbury Cathedral accompanied by Jethro Tull while the great Irish tenor John McCormack sings it with his distinctive Irish accent as a conventional ballad in a recording made in 1941. Fat Les sang it as a football anthem accompanied by the London Gay Men's Choir and Eric Idle sang it on *Monty Python's Flying Circus*.[17] No one will ever own *Jerusalem*. It is a song constantly reinvented and reinterpreted by different groups and singers, each having their own furrow to plough.

And the finest rendition of this great song? That will always be a matter of personal opinion, but for this writer, it has to be that sung by Paul Robeson. This African American was famous as the singer of *Ole Man River* from *Showboat* but Robeson was also an actor who portrayed Othello and many other iconic black figures on stage. He lived in England for several years and was the first black person to read the lesson at Saint Paul's Cathedral.[18] As he did so he was standing just a few yards above where the original composer of *Jerusalem*, Hubert Parry, is buried and where William Blake is commemorated. Robeson was the son of a man who had escaped from slavery, while Blake drew pictures for and supported the abolitionist movement in England. Blake raged against mental enslavement while Robeson was a tireless campaigner for civil rights who stood up to McCarthyism. Listen to Robeson's deep baritone voice singing Blake's words and you will hear a connection across the centuries that reminds you that, while *Jerusalem* may be a patriotic song, it should never be a complacent one.

Notes

1. olympic.org/news/London-2012-publishes-its-final-report-and-accounts
2. You can view the full ceremony on YouTube (youtube.com/watch?=4Aoe4de-rl)
3. iainsinclair.org.uk/2011/07/09/iainsinclair-the-olympics-have-destroyed-my-patch-of-london-interview-on-the-independent
4. Quoted from an article on Blake in *The Guardian* 21 October 2000 by Neil Spencer
5. statista.com/statistics/294729/population-united-kingdom-by-country/
6. bbc.co.uk/news/uk-england-51646140
7. barmyarmy.com
8. nrl.com/operations/history-of-rugby-league/
9. brightmorningstar.org/why-do-they-sing-abide-with-me-at fa-cup-finals/
10. From an email to the author.
11. There are two versions of Chris Dann playing *Jerusalem* on the piano on YouTube, the first a conventional rendition of Parry's tune, the second a jazzier version. To view them go to youtube.com and search for "Jerusalem Chris Dann."
12. Various versions of Billy Bragg singing *Jerusalem* can be seen on YouTube. To view them go to youtube.com and search for "Jerusalem Billy Bragg."
13. Article in *The Guardian* 18 February 2009
14. Article in *The Guardian* 17 December 2019
15. From an email to the author
16. *The Three Dimensions of Freedom* by Billy Bragg, Faber and Faber, 2019 (page 41). Bragg's number one hit was his 1988 version of the Beatles' *She's Leaving Home*.
17. In the sketch *Owl Stretching Time*
18. Thanks to Angela Morgan for his information.

Chapter 10

Remembering the Writers

Elgar's Hideaway

No one knows why it is called Hallelujah Corner. The name goes back at least to 1945 when a photograph of the junction was taken[1] so it cannot be a tribute to the song by Leonard Cohen, which was written in 1984. It may be because there used to be a church there; it may be because it is a potentially dangerous corner and you could be heading up to Heaven if you are not careful turning into it; or it may simply be that, when you finally find it, you breathe a sigh of relief and mutter "hallelujah" in the sense of "at last" instead of "thanks be to God".

The junction is on the A283 between Pulborough and Petworth and, as you turn right, you head up a narrow but still paved road through an area of woodland towards the village of Bedham. If you go as far as the village you will have passed Brinkwells, the house where Edward Elgar spent most of his time between 1917 and 1919 and where he enjoyed a late flowering of creativity. Look out for a wooden sign on the right-hand side of the road as you come to the brow of the hill about two miles from the main road. On this sign, the single word "Brinkwells" is carved. Blink and you will miss it (as this author did when first attempting to find the house). Brinkwells is privately owned now and not open to the public.

The studio where Elgar did most of his writing – and where he may well have written the score for *Jerusalem* – can be seen about a mile further up the road where you can see grass growing out of the tarmac. The road forks here and one branch declines steeply towards a series of elegant and spacious houses made of stone, some with thatched roofs. The little black wooden hut where Elgar worked (and which helpfully has the words "The

Studio" inscribed on it) stands at this fork. It was transported here from Brinkwells in 1929 and a spacious house was built next to it which you can see – and even live in if you are so inclined. Although the studio is quite small, the house sleeps up to eight people and comes equipped with a dishwasher, wood-burning stove, washing machine and, essential to attract customers today, wifi.[2]

Elgar's wife Alice had discovered Brinkwells and felt, correctly as it turned out, that it would suit her talented but sometimes listless husband. She herself did not care that much for life in the cottage and preferred Severn House, their large home in Hampstead, the only home they purchased during their married life. It was in Severn House that she died in 1920 and, although the widowed Elgar returned to Brinkwells in 1921 and even offered to buy the lease from the Reverend Vicat Cole, from whom they had rented the house, life there was not the same without Alice. He left Sussex and returned to London and then went to live in his native Worcestershire, where he is buried next to his wife.

Elgar had enjoyed the isolation of Brinkwells and responded with his final burst of creativity inspired by the peace it afforded him. He was more at home in the green and pleasant land than amongst the dark satanic mills and it was at Brinkwells that he wrote a Violin Sonata, a String Quartet, a Piano Quintet and the Cello Concerto, made famous in the film *Hilary and Jackie*. He probably also wrote the score for his setting of *Jerusalem* here, as it was first performed at the Leeds Music Festival in 1922 soon after he left Brinkwells for the final time. He had called his cottage: "divine … a simple thatched cottage and a (soiled) studio with a wonderful view: large garden unweeded, a task for 40 men".[3]

The move to Sussex from London led to both an improvement in Elgar's physical health as well as this outpouring of creative energy. In the Sussex woodlands, he convalesced from his throat operation, chopped wood and composed music. A frequent visitor was his friend the violinist W H (Billy) Reed, who worked with Elgar on his compositions and later recalled: "All the music composed at Brinkwells was undoubtedly influenced by the quiet and peaceful surroundings during that wonderful summer (1918). Miles of woodland, through which he walked daily enchanted him by their beauty and serenity. How truly he could translate these moods and feelings into music."[4] The miles of woodland are still there and the walker who prefers the shelter of the woods to the well-trodden and exposed South Downs Way nearby can still walk through them. This area is part of the South Downs National Park, created in 2010 as England's newest national park.

Elgar loved the solitude of this area and liked to go walking in the woods where his creative juices could flow. Visitors like Reed would arrive occasionally and either be squeezed into the cottage or stay at the nearby Swan Inn. The Elgars, however, retained Severn House in Hampstead and Alice would return there every so often and leave her husband to his own musical and rural devices at Brinkwells. In an echo of Catherine Blake's attitude to the cottage in Felpham, Lady Elgar seemed to prefer the comforts of the big city to rural isolation in Sussex. The Elgars could afford to move between these two homes – unlike the Blakes, who often struggled to pay the rent on one house, let alone two.

Whereas Catherine Blake outlived her husband by several years, it was Alice Elgar who died first. In over thirty years of marriage, she had stood by Elgar and aided his musical ambitions and been a supportive but informed critic of his work. She knew that he liked young women near him who could act as muses but she was never possessive or jealous. There might be periods when they were apart, as he preferred the country while she was more at home in the city. On occasions, Elgar would visit his sister, to whom he was close, but Alice would not join them, as she had little in common with his family. However, she never let the difference in age, class or interests come between them. Elgar did move back to Brinkwells for a time in 1921 but, without his wife to look after him and keep him company, life there was not the same. Cole was unwilling to sell the lease and, feeling lonely after Alice's death, Elgar's creative fires subsided and it was mostly silent during the last years of his life.

After Elgar left, Brinkwells too began to subside and fall into ruin. In 1929, eight years after he had last used it for composition, the studio was moved a mile up the hill to its present location and a house was built next to it in 1929, later extended in 1949. It was here that *Elgar's Tenth Muse*, a television film about him was made in which Edward Fox, who bears a fair resemblance to the composer, starred as Elgar. The house by the studio was once occupied by the late Reginald Bosanquet, a journalist who was notorious for his love of a drink. Some people may remember him reading the ten o'clock news on ITV opposite Anna Ford, sometimes in a tired and emotional condition.

This part of Sussex has always boasted a fair number of artistic and creative types amongst its residents. At around the time that Bosanquet was living in the large house next to the studio, Brinkwells itself was occupied by Robert Walker, a composer and musician, some of whose works are homages to Elgar or completed versions of those he left unfinished. These include a late Piano Concerto that Walker imagined into completion and which was given a sympathetic review by Gramophone Magazine and performed on BBC radio.[5] Walker breathed in the spirit of Elgar at Brinkwells and restored the house but has since moved away. It is now a privately owned family home and is not to the public.

The very remoteness of Elgar's Sussex cottage makes it hard to find. For one of his visitors, Elgar drew a map complete with a portrait of himself with moustache, hat, walking stick and even his dog Meg. He draws "the smoke of welcome" at the cottage and adds the message "we have coal". He signed the map "Edward Elgar, Cartographer". However, Elgar's cartographical skills did not prove of much use to this particular visitor, who tried to use the map to walk to the nearby Pulborough train station and an hour later came back to exactly where he had set off from![6] From this homemade map you gain a glimpse of the lighter-hearted Elgar than the melancholy figure he is often portrayed as. Although he did not spend much of his life in Sussex, Brinkwells was to be the last place he lived where his creative juices flowed freely and where he probably – it is not possible to speak with more certainty – made his small but telling contribution to the story of *Jerusalem*.

* * *

Parry – worth a plaque

Of the three houses in the Sussex triangle occupied by the creators of *Jerusalem*, the largest and most comfortable must be Knightscroft House, the home of Hubert Parry, his wife and their two daughters. It is only five-minute walk from the English Channel in the village of Rustington, roughly halfway between Bognor Regis and Worthing. The house is divided into flats and is not open to the public. The only indication that Parry lived there is the blue plaque on a stone near the front entrance.

Knightscroft House is a Grade two listed building designed for Parry by the Scottish architect Norman Shaw in 1879.[7] Shaw is best known for the building usually called New Scotland Yard on the Thames Embankment in London. The name of his most famous building, on the wall of which you can see a medallion with Shaw's profile, has nothing to do with his Scottish origins but derives from the fact that the headquarters of London's police force was originally located in Great Scotland Yard off Whitehall. This was effectively the Scottish Embassy in London for many years, when England and Scotland were separate countries with different royal families. The police have long moved out of the original Scotland Yard but they took the famous name with them, one familiar to most visitors to London, particularly those who enjoy the *Sherlock Holmes* stories of Arthur Conan Doyle.

Shaw, like his near-contemporary Edwin Lutyens, was a working architect who combined designing prestigious buildings with the more lucrative business of providing private homes for people who knew his name through the public work he undertook. Parry's commission came fairly early in Shaw's career, soon after he had established his own architectural practice. Parry too had gone his own way and committed himself to earning a living from music having left his position as a Lloyds underwriter, one he found neither fulfilling nor particularly lucrative. He evidently had money as he could afford to commission Shaw to build this substantial house and bring his wife and daughters, Dorothea and Gwendoline, to live there. They were named after the two Brooke sisters in George Eliot's novel *Middlemarch*. Paying homage to this popular but unconventional Victorian writer, who was openly living with a married man and was known to be a doubter in religious matters, gives a fair indication of Parry's own scepticism when it came to the teachings of the church.

Unlike George Eliot, however, Parry could not afford to be openly hostile towards conventional Christian morality as much of his work would be performed in a church setting. He lived a life of conventional propriety, moving between his London home in Kensington near to the Royal College of Music and Rustington in Sussex. It was in Rustington where he entertained people like James Barrie, the author of *Peter Pan*. Barrie was friendly with the Llewellyn Davies family who was the inspiration behind the family in his famous story. An old photograph shows him playing cricket in Rustington with Earl Haig, who is holding a bat wearing his full military uniform.

The Llewellyn Davies family were close to Parry's daughter Dorothea, whose own daughter Elizabeth was one of the "bright young things", the smart aristocratic set of the 1920s and 30s portrayed by writers like Evelyn Waugh.

A local history book[8] says that Rustington later became quite a hotbed of British fascism. The vicar James Crosland and his son John were enthusiastic members of Oswald Mosley's black-shirts and, as headmaster of the local school, Crosland Senior attempted to inculcate the children there with the message that Hitler was "trying to do what he could to make Europe a much better place and he should be admired and respected as a wonderful leader". The Croslands were also friends of William Joyce, who was often seen in the village. He is better known as Lord Haw Haw from his broadcasts during the Second World War, and was later hanged for dispersing Nazi propaganda. Both Parry and Blake would have despaired at the way Hitler and Mosley became popular figures in the brief heyday of British fascism before the German version became the enemy during the Second World War.

Parry's comfortable home Knightscroft House is now divided into four flats, worth around a quarter of a million pounds each.[9] In addition, there are some small flats in what were servant's quarters when the building was originally constructed. A helpful lady showed the author around the outside of the house, but he was not invited inside. These are private homes occupied mostly, she indicated, by elderly people who did not wish to be disturbed.[10] An Englishman's home is his (or more probably, in Rustington, her) castle, after all.

Although I was unable to enter Knightscroft House, I did receive an invitation to Shulbrede Priory which is where Parry's daughter Dorothea and her husband Arthur Ponsonby lived and is now the home of Ian Russell and his wife Kate, who is Parry's great-granddaughter. The house outdoes Knightscroft by being Grade One listed and is over eight hundred years old, a delightfully dilapidated old building near Haslemere just across the Surrey-Sussex border. Shulbrede is not normally open to the public but the Russells were hospitable enough to invite me to see their collection of Parry memorabilia. I was able to see – and even hold – the original score of *Jerusalem* and to see the diary entry in which Parry blithely notes, "Wrote a tune for some words of Blake's which Bridges sent me," before writing the next day that he "Made a tidy copy of the tune to Blake's stanzas", adding "Weather damp and cold". As Samuel Johnson famously said, when two Englishmen meet they talk of the weather. It seems that Parry did not even need the company of another to note what it was like.

Parry often visited his daughter and her husband at Shulbrede and even wrote some *Shulbrede Tunes*, musical portraits of members of the family. He is remembered in the family as an enthusiastic grandparent, who would hide from his grandchildren under the table and rarely tired of playing games with them. The house has several photographs of Parry and one of their treasures is a maquette of the composer, a small statuette intended as a model for a proposed statue of him that would stand outside the Royal College of Music. Despite Prince Charles's championship of his favourite composer, however, this statue has never been erected. It costs a good six-figure sum to commission and erect a public statue these days and Hubert Parry sadly does not command that sort of money. A campaign to honour Jack Leslie, a black British footballer of the 1920s who was due to play for England but was denied a cap simply because of his skin colour, needed to raise a hundred thousand pounds to do honour this early victim of racism. They ended up exceeding their target and Leslie will be commemorated in Plymouth, where he played.

Parry is worth a plaque, it would seem, but not famous enough for a statue or museum. Elgar's name is familiar to many and is used to attract residents to where he scored Parry's tune but Brinkwells is too remote and inaccessible to be turned into a tourist attraction. In any case, there is already a museum dedicated to Elgar at the Firs, the house in Worcestershire where he was born.[11] Only Shakespeare and Dickens have more than one building dedicated to preserving their memory and Elgar, despite being probably the finest composer to come from "the land without music", is not quite in that league.

William Blake, on the other hand ...

* * *

Bugger Bognor

Of the three creators of *Jerusalem* – Blake, Parry and Elgar – it was the London-based engraver, artist and poet William Blake who would be most surprised to find that the song he contributed the words to has become a second national anthem for England, sung by crowds of people attending political conferences, sporting occasions or Women's Institute meetings. *Jerusalem* is sung by professionals and amateurs, at classical concerts and by rock groups, at weddings and funerals, at royal occasions and by staunch republicans. It is loved by members of the establishment and by revolutionaries who want to overthrow that same establishment. Truly, the appeal of this most English song is almost universal.

Yet the man who wrote the words we sing was above all an individual, an eccentric whom many of his contemporaries considered to be insane. Until his later years, when he was surrounded by people who admired and accepted him, William Blake found it hard to maintain friendships and to remain on good terms with other people, many of whom had tried to help him achieve a small measure of the popular success he now enjoys. He had a strong marriage to Catherine but this was a relationship in which the woman was subservient to and respectful of her husband, which adds a certain irony to the way his words were adopted by female suffragists a hundred years after he wrote them.

The words of Blake's poem contrast the green and pleasant land of an idyllic England with the dark satanic mills of the industrial revolution taking place as he wrote it. Although it is usually taken as read that Blake was celebrating the countryside rather than the city, he and Catherine returned to London after barely two years in Felpham. This had been the only time the Blakes had lived outside the capital and the Scofield incident, while it contributed to their desire to leave, was more a symptom of the way they were considered outsiders than the cause of their flight back to more familiar territory. It is hard not to conclude that the Blakes were more at home amongst those mills than in close proximity to the green land where people may not have been particularly pleasant to them. The reality of life in rural England could never live up to the Jerusalem of Blake's imagination.

In the city, Blake could busy himself with his work, scratch around for clients and, if not always comfortable with those around him, he would at least be accepted as a fairly harmless eccentric by his neighbours and acquaintances. In London, people come and go, moving house as the Blakes often did, and there would be a wide variety of those he could do business and interact with. Radical ideas, which he often espoused, might be more readily tolerated in the big city than in a small village. "He is a little odd, Mister Blake, but harmless enough," you can imagine people in London saying of him.

This would be less likely in Felpham. People in a village can be suspicious of outsiders, particularly those who bring their big city ways and new-fangled ideas with them. You are expected to doff your cap to your social superiors – anathema to a proud and independent man like Blake – and to accept that things are done in a certain way, as they have been for centuries. You are surrounded by a small number of people in a village and, if they do not take to you, it can seem very lonely.

While the people in Blake's Felpham would have made their living mostly from farming and other predominantly rural occupations, the village today is more of a home to those who have already made their money. Around ten thousand people live there, many of them in gated communities or detached houses with expensive cars parked outside. Although it is administratively independent, Felpham has in practice been absorbed into and acts as a suburb of Bognor Regis, a resort town on the south made famous for being the site of one of Billy Butlin's first holiday camps. Bognor, like several southern resorts, has a pier and a string of ice cream and fish and chip shops along its seafront.

In Blake's day, it was plain Bognor, the "Regis" being added to commemorate the convalescence there of King George V in 1929. According to popular legend, when the king was on his deathbed at Sandringham House in 1935, his doctor suggested that he might soon be well enough to revisit the town, to which he pithily replied "Bugger Bognor" and then conked out. This shows a more human side to this irascible monarch than his official last words, "How is the empire?" In fact, he had probably uttered the phrase some years earlier when he first established his views on the town. As Blake and his wife packed their few possessions and his precious engraving tools up in order to return to London, it is not hard to imagine him uttering a similar sentiment to the Queen's grandfather.

Yet it was not always like this. In a letter to John's Flaxman wife, written soon after the move to Felpham, Blake included a poem encouraging the couple to visit Felpham:

This song to the flower of Flaxman's joy,
To the blossom of hope for a sweet decoy;
Do all that you can, or all that you may,
To entice him to Felpham and far away.

Away to sweet Felpham for Heaven is there;
The Ladder of Angels descends thro' the air;
On the turret it spiral does softly descend,
Thro' the village then winds, at my cot it does end.

You stand in the village and look up to Heaven;
The precious stones glitter on flights seventy-seven;
And my brother is there, and my friend and thine
Descend and ascend with the bread and the wine.

The bread of sweet thought and wine of delight
Feed the village of Felpham by day and by night,
And at his own door the bless'd Hermit does stand,
Dispensing unceasing to all the wind land.[12]

The "hermit" is Blake's patron William Hayley who lived in a large house nearby surmounted by the turret mentioned in the second verse. The sentiment expressed in the first two lines of the final stanza is quoted on a sign near the cottage to show what Blake felt of Felpham. The poem in the letter was written, however, in 1800 soon after the Blakes arrived and long before the Scofield incident which led to their hasty return to London. Although he spent only two of his three score and ten years on earth in the Felpham cottage, it is there that Blake is to be commemorated through the rebuilding and reopening of the cottage where he and Catherine lived. Tim Heath is Chair of the Blake Cottage Trust and he is keen to see the cottage restored. He takes inspiration for the Blake Cottage project from the plan to convert Derek Jarman's Prospect Cottage in Dungeness into a homage to the filmmaker who died of Aids in 1994.[13] The Jarman campaign has raised three and a half million pounds to restore both the building and Jarman's beloved garden.[14]

In some ways Jarman was a twentieth century Blake, a comparison he would have been flattered by (and which probably occurred to him). Both men worked in various art forms without ever trimming their sails for commercial success. They had a strong individualistic vision and were regarded as outsiders, oddballs even, during their lifetimes. Both Blake and Jarman lived next to the sea in houses which are being converted to commemorate them and, while Jarman made his home in a small fisherman's cottage in Kent, Blake stayed in a larger thatched house in Sussex. It is here in Sussex, rather than his native London, that the Blake Society plans to remember one of England's unlikeliest heroes.[15]

The house at Blake's Road is one of an estimated fifty to sixty thousand thatched buildings in England.[16] Since 1928, it had belonged to the family of Heather Howell who told Tim Heath that she hoped that "one day it should go into trust for all those who are inspired by Blake."[17] After the last of the Howell family had died, the Blake Society set about raising the money to fulfil her wish. The house had not been left to the Society so the money had to be raised to purchase it. Many lovers of Blake, in the words of Tim Heath, "eschew money" but they have donated various amounts. The Sainsburys Monument Trust gave £25,000; West Sussex County Council and the National Lottery Heritage Fund each donated £10,000 and the Mercer's Company gave £2,000. The largest individual donation, however, was an anonymous one which consisted of £400,000, over three-quarters of the sum needed. In all, there were 743 contributors ranging from one pound upwards.[18] If it had not been for that large and anonymous donation, however, it is unlikely the project would have been able to proceed. Even so, the cottage was classified as "at risk" by Historic England in late 2021.

Restoration is proceeding now even if there is little sign of obvious activity when you look at the house. It is still standing not far from the seaside in Felpham, with local flint and bricks in its walls, a thatched roof and a decent-sized garden. On an open day in 2018, I went along to examine what was happening and spoke to various people involved with the cottage. The feeling was – very strongly – that they did not want the museum and gift shop type of centre that so many writers like Shakespeare, Dickens and Wordsworth are honoured with, but something closer to the spirit of Blake himself. The cottage would be converted into a study centre and a place to live for artistic and creative people, the true heirs of William Blake being given an opportunity to express themselves creatively without being overwhelmed by the demands of commerce.

There is still some way to go, however. Visitors could see that work had been done and architectural plans drawn up for the new centre. Plaster and timberwork from the old building were exposed as the conversion process from a family home to a study centre continued. I was reminded of Blake's curiously ungrammatical word "builded", which occurs in the second stanza of the poem just before "these dark satanic mills". It should, of course, be "built" but the word does not scan properly and so Blake simply added the second syllable, creating a previously unknown but strangely appropriate word in the process. Building a good rhythm was more important to him than mere grammatical accuracy – and he may well have sung the lines himself to Catherine and others to now lost music.

At the time of writing the new centre has not been completed. Blake has a new grave next to Catherine at Bunhill Fields and a monument. He has memorials at both Westminster Abbey and Saint Paul's Cathedral. His words are sung every year by Women's Institutes, sports lovers and the audience at the Last Night of the Proms. All that remains is for the cottage where he wrote the words of Jerusalem to be restored in his memory. That, in his own word, is still to be builded.

Notes

1. Available from sussexpictures.co.uk
2. Go to amberleyhousecottages.co.uk to see photographs and

book a stay at the house.

Elgar, Vicat Cole and the Ghosts of Brinkwells by Carol Fitzgerald and Brian W Harvey (pages 47/8)

3. Article in *Sussex Life* magazine, October 2019, by Richard Westwood-Brookes (Available on pressreader.com/uk/sussex-life/20191001/282106343364660)
4. gramophone.co.uk/review/elgarwalker-piano-concerto-other-orchestral-works
5. Fitzgerald Harvey
6. historicengland.org.uk/listing/the-list/list-entry/1027592
7. *Winds of Change in a Sleepy Sussex Village* by Graeme and Mary Taylor
8. Prices estimated from zoopla.co.uk property website
9. The lady who showed me the house preferred to remain anonymous.
10. The house is maintained by the National Trust. For opening times and prices go to:
11. nationaltrust.org.uk/the-firs.
12. The poem is from a letter to Anna Flaxman, September 1800
13. Conversation with the author, September 2020.
14. Go to: artfund.org/get-involved/art-happens/prospect-cottage for details and donations.
15. Go to blakecottage.org for details and donations.
16. Thanks to Andrew Raffle, Secretary of the National Society of Master Thatchers
17. blakesociety.org/blakecottage/
18. Figures from accounts published at blakesociety.org/blakecottage/

Author Biography

Edwin Lerner is a tourist guide and writer who has long been fascinated with the story of England's second national anthem *Jerusalem*. He has often taken groups to Glastonbury, where King Arthur is reputedly buried, and accompanies parties from every part of the world around Britain and Ireland. He has written three books and several articles on tourist guiding and travel and prides himself on conducting tours through every part of Britain and Ireland. The only tours he will not run are those concerned with Jack the Ripper.

Edwin writes his own weekly blog on guiding matters, prepares posts for the Guide London website and edits a monthly magazine for guides called, unsurprisingly, Guidelines, a name he claims to have invented.

Previous Titles

Walk This Way (Bank House Books, 2005) was Edwin's first book on tourist guiding which looks at various aspects of the tourism business.

The Guide Book (Blueprint Press, 2007) contains a series of facts and information designed for the curious visitor to Britain and Ireland.

Even the Old Bags Laughed is a series of anecdotes about Edwin's life as a tourist guide which he hoped to persuade an editor and then a publisher to take up. Sadly, this did not happen but the stories subtitled *110 Tales from the Travel Trade* is available as an ebook.

Note to reader

Thank you for buying *Jerusalem – The Story of a Song*. Please feel free to add your review of the book at your favourite online site for feedback. You are welcome to visit my website: eddielernertourguide.co.uk or to read my weekly blog at diaryofatouristguide.blogspot.com. I post every Monday on matters that interest me and I do not carry advertising on either site.

Abbreviations

Very few abbreviations are used in the text and most of these are fairly well known:

BBC – British Broadcasting Corporation

NHS – National Health Service

WI – Women's Institute.

Bibliography

Akroyd, Peter, *William Blake*, Vintage, 1996 (Isbn 9780749391768)

Aldous, Richard, *Tunes Of Glory: The Life of Malcolm Sargent*, Pimlico, 2001 (ISBN 0-7126-6540-4)

Boyle, David, *Jerusalem*, Ebook

Bragg, Billy, *The Three Dimensions Of Freedom*, Faber and Faber, 2019 (ISBN 978-0-571-35321-7)

Breverton, Terry *The King In The Car Park*, Amberley Publishing, 2013 (ISBN 9781445621050)

Concannon, Amy and Myrone, Martin *William Blake*, Tate Publishing, 2019 (ISBN 978 1 84976 6333 3)

Deane Tony and Shaw, Tony, *Folklore of Cornwall*, History Press, 2009 (ISBN 9780752429298)

Dibble, Jeremy, *C Hubert Parry, His Life And Music*, Oxford University Press, 1992 (ISBN 0-19-315330-0)

Doctor Jenny and Wright, David (eds,) *The Proms: A New History*, Thames and Hudson, 2007 (ISBN-13: 978-0-500-51352-1 ISBN-10: 0-500-5132-X)

Farley, Paul and Simmons, Michael Roberts, *Deaths of the Poets*, Jonathan Cape, 2017 (ISBN 9780224097543)

Fitzgerald, Carol and Harvey, Brian W, *Elgar, Vicat Cole and the Ghosts Of Brinkwells*, Phillimore, 2007 (ISBN 978-1-86077-442-3)

Northrop Moore, Jerrold, *Edward Elgar, A Creative Life*, Oxford University Press, 1984 (ISBN (0-19-315447-I)

Stenson, W H, (ed), *William Blake: The Complete Poems*, text by David V Erdman, Longman, 1971 (ISBN 0 582 48459 6)

Stewart, Tricia, *Calendar Girl*, Northern Angel, 2017 (ISBN 978-1-527205-82-6)

Taylor, Graeme and Mary, *Winds of Change in a Sleepy Sussex Village (Rustington)*, Writersworld, 2015 (ISBN 978-0-9933555-0-9)

Tester, Angela, *The Suffragettes at Littlehampton*, Museum Booklet

CHRONOS
BOOKS

HISTORY

Chronos Books is an historical non-fiction imprint. Chronos publishes real history for real people; bringing to life people, places and events in an imaginative, easy-to-digest and accessible way - histories that pass on their stories to a generation of new readers.
If you have enjoyed this book, why not tell other readers by posting a review on your preferred book site.

Recent bestsellers from Chronos Books are:

Lady Katherine Knollys
The Unacknowledged Daughter of King Henry VIII
Sarah-Beth Watkins
A comprehensive account of Katherine Knollys' questionable paternity, her previously unexplored life in the Tudor court and her intriguing relationship with Elizabeth I.
Paperback: 978-1-78279-585-8 ebook: 978-1-78279-584-1

Cromwell was Framed
Ireland 1649
Tom Reilly
Revealed: The definitive research that proves the Irish nation
owes Oliver Cromwell a huge posthumous apology for
wrongly convicting him of civilian atrocities in 1649.
Paperback: 978-1-78279-516-2 ebook: 978-1-78279-515-5

Why The CIA Killed JFK and Malcolm X
The Secret Drug Trade in Laos
John Koerner
A new groundbreaking work presenting evidence that the CIA
silenced JFK to protect its secret drug trade in Laos.
Paperback: 978-1-78279-701-2 ebook: 978-1-78279-700-5

The Disappearing Ninth Legion
A Popular History
Mark Olly
The Disappearing Ninth Legion examines hard evidence for the
foundation, development, mysterious disappearance, or possi-
ble continuation of Rome's lost Legion.
Paperback: 978-1-84694-559-5 ebook: 978-1-84694-931-9

Beaten But Not Defeated
Siegfried Moos - A German anti-Nazi who settled in Britain
Merilyn Moos
Siegi Moos, an anti-Nazi and active member of the German
Communist Party, escaped Germany in 1933 and, exiled in
Britain, sought another route to the transformation
of capitalism.
Paperback: 978-1-78279-677-0 ebook: 978-1-78279-676-3

A Schoolboy's Wartime Letters
An evacuee's life in WWII — A Personal Memoir
Geoffrey Iley
A boy writes home during WWII, revealing his own fascinating story, full of zest for life, information and humour.
Paperback: 978-1-78279-504-9 ebook: 978-1-78279-503-2

The Life & Times of the Real Robyn Hoode
Mark Olly
A journey of discovery. The chronicles of the genuine historical character, Robyn Hoode, and how he became one of England's greatest legends.
Paperback: 978-1-78535-059-7 ebook: 978-1-78535-060-3

Readers of ebooks can buy or view any of these bestsellers by clicking on the live link in the title. Most titles are published in paperback and as an ebook. Paperbacks are available in traditional bookshops. Both print and ebook formats are available online.

Find more titles and sign up to our readers' newsletter at
http://www.johnhuntpublishing.com/history-home

Follow us on Facebook at
https://www.facebook.com/ChronosBooks

and Twitter at https://twitter.com/ChronosBooks